HOUSES IN FINLAND

Harri Hautajärvi

HOUSES IN FINLAND

Rakennustieto Publishing, Helsinki

Finnland-Institut in Deutschland
für Kultur, Wissenschaft und
Wirtschaft GmbH (gemeinnützig)
Georgenstraße 24, 10117 Berlin
Telefon +49-30-520 02 60 10
Telefax +49-30-520 02 60 29
www.finnland-institut.de

Publisher
Rakennustieto Publishing
www.rakennustieto.fi
P.O. Box 1004
00101 Helsinki
Finland
phone + 358 207 4 76 4 00

Editor
Harri Hautajärvi

Editor for Rakennustieto Publishing
Kristiina Bergholm

Translation from Finnish and language consulting
Kristina Kölhi and Gareth Griffiths / Gekko

Graphic design
Jussi Vuori / JADA

Paper
Gallerie Art Silk 150 g

Typeface
Gotham / Hoefler & Frere-Jones

Printers
Kolofon OÜ, Estonia 2011

Cover photos
Front cover: Villa Aamutuuli (Jari Jetsonen)
Back cover: Kekkapää House (Antti Hahl), Villa Lena (Jussi Tiainen), Into House (Jyrki Tasa), Studio Widnäs (Rauno Träskelin)

© Authors and Rakennustieto Oy

ISBN 978-951-682-947-3 (this edition)
ISBN 978-951-682-988-6 (Finnish edition, *Omakotitaloja*)

CONTENTS

6	Preface
8	A house of one's own – a Finnish dream
40	**Studio Widnäs**	TUOMO SIITONEN
50	**Villa Lena**	OLAVI KOPONEN
58	**Kotilo House**	OLAVI KOPONEN
66	**Tammimäki House**	MATTI AND PIRJO SANAKSENAHO
72	**Laulumaa House**	LAURI LOUEKARI
76	**Foni House**	ANNA AND LAURI LOUEKARI
80	**Villa Lepola**	JUHA LEIVISKÄ AND TAPANI SCHRODERUS
86	**Sjöboda House**	JUHA LEIVISKÄ AND ROSEMARIE SCHNITZLER
90	**Moby Dick**	JYRKI TASA AND TUOMAS UUSHEIMO
96	**Into House**	JYRKI TASA
102	**Eriksson House**	HEIKKI AITOAHO AND KAARLO VILJANEN
106	**Villa Smedjebacka**	HEIKKI AITOAHO AND KAARLO VILJANEN
112	**Melin House**	HEIKKI AITOAHO AND KAARLO VILJANEN
116	**Kekkapää House**	KATARIINA RAUTIALA AND PENTTI RAISKI
124	**Päivärinne House**	SANTERI LIPASTI
134	**Villa Aamutuuli**	ASKO KINNUNEN
140	**Villa Inkeri**	HANNU KIISKILÄ
144	**Villa Sari**	HANNU KIISKILÄ
148	**Versta House**	TITTA TAMMINEN AND JUHANI KARANKA
154	**Alanen House**	TAPANI MUSTONEN
160	**Saddler's cottage**	KRISTIAN GULLICHSEN AND JYRI HAUKKAVAARA
166	**Villa Pajumäki**	JUHA ILONEN
170	**Hienovirta House**	YRJÄNÄ VUOJALA
174	**Toivio House**	TEEMU TOIVIO
180	**Humlegård House**	KIMMO FRIMAN
188	**Villa Kari**	OLAVI KOPONEN
194	**Koti House**	HEIKKI VIIRI
198	**Wiima House**	HEIKKI VIIRI
202	**Holappa House**	PAVE MIKKONEN
206	**3 Trees House**	PAVE MIKKONEN
210	**"Touch" House**	MIKKO HEIKKINEN AND MARKKU KOMONEN
216	**Domus Arborea**	VESA PEKKA ERIKKILÄ AND MARJUT KAUPPINEN
220	**Villa Niinimäki**	TEIJU AUTIO AND SEEPO SEROLA

Villa Hemstrand stands proudly on a shoreline plot in Västervik, Vaasa. The wooden house designed by Heikki Aitoaho and Kaarlo Viljanen was built in 2005.

PREFACE

Today, at the same time as the desire to live in a more natural way has become more popular and saving energy has become a virtue, there has also been a growing interest in home interior decoration and the architectural design of dwellings.

In the design of single-family houses one can perhaps see most clearly what is considered quintessential Finnish architecture: natural materials, wood surfaces, minimalist modernism and a life lived close to nature. Although a single-family house could, due to its small size, be perceived as a simple design task, building regulations and increasingly stricter energy efficiency requirements have made it ever more demanding. Sustainable construction entails the coordination of numerous factors, including the natural conditions of the plot, the energy-saving form and envelope of the building, self-sufficiency in energy production, a long life cycle, as well as local and renewable building materials.

This book is a compilation of what I regard as the best of Finnish single-family house architecture from recent years, featuring 33 individually designed homes. Each house is presented through photographs and drawings as well as a text written by the architect him- or herself. I intentionally chose a varied selection of houses occupied by different people with different incomes to give an idea of the architectural diversity of Finnish single-family houses.

These houses differ from both mainstream single-family houses and from each other; they come in different sizes and shapes because the architects have designed them according to the occupants' wishes.

The book presents a wide selection from the range of Finnish architecture in terms of form and style through imaginative and personal solutions, applications relying on tradition, and beautiful and practical, and bright and stylish spaces. The buildings have been skillfully positioned on their plots, safeguarding the surrounding trees. The floor plans are functional and natural light is utilised in the different interior spaces in the most appropriate way. The connections to the surrounding garden, yard or landscape are natural, and at their best the exterior and interior spaces interweave with each other.

In the introductory article I tell about the long history of Finnish single-family house design, about the changes in the culture of dwelling and about sustainable construction principles.

This book is so far the most extensive book on the architecture of Finnish single-family houses. It provides useful information and practical beauty for all those interested in such houses, be they owners, those who dream of owning such a house as well as designers and students in the building profession.

Harri Hautajärvi

A HOUSE OF ONE'S OWN – A FINNISH DREAM

Ideas about the pursuit of happiness and a better quality of life inevitably come to mind when looking at contemporary single-family houses and their treatment by the media and marketing. The design solutions for dwellings and interior decoration play a more important role than ever before in Western life, and a large part of people's income is spent on them. Opportunities for self-expression are increasingly available and this is also reflected in the advertising directed at people's lifestyles and the interior decoration of their homes.

In Finland the ideal dwelling for most people is a house of one's own set on a quiet garden plot – and a similar dream home exists, naturally, in many other countries, too. On the global scale, however, a single-family house fitted with all modern conveniences is quite rare, but the norm in Finland. Indeed, currently about 55 per cent of the Finnish population lives in a single-family house. The area of Finland is comparatively large but sparsely populated: 5.3 million people inhabit an area close to the size of Germany, and with an average population density of only 17 people per square kilometre.

Finland is a country of contrasts. Located at the northern periphery of Europe, it is for many a relatively unknown country, and hence some people associate it with funny myths, such as it being continuously cold, that the people are quiet and tenacious, and that polarbears wander the streets. Although Finns are modest and reluctant to praise themselves, recent studies have shown a picture of the nation quite different than even we Finns could have imagined. For instance, in international studies and comparisons, Finland has been selected as, among other things, "the best country in the world", and Finns the third happiest nation in Europe. Finland has been identified as one of the world's best democracies, one of the least corrupt countries, and among the leading countries in gender equality. Finnish students are often placed first in the world when measuring schoolchildren's competence.[1] The Finnish egalitarian society has been built up over a long period, with measures such as, for instance, the levelling of the distribution of incomes and free education and healthcare.

Although Finland today has become more pluralistic and the people to a large extent more individualistic, one can still find cultural characteristics that unite the nation. In a country where the mobile phone was developed into a worldwide hit product, people spend time with social media but also spend quality time outdoors. They are active in different ways, in the forest and on the sea. Some enjoy plunging themselves into a hole in the ice after emerging from a hot sauna. And all these same people may very well also be active users of their local library. The contemporary Finnish way of life combines a high standard of living, a high level of education

A summer moment captured in the garden of Villa Ervi at the beginning of the 1950s. Aarne Ervi worked on the design of his own family house on the island of Kuusisaari from 1939 onwards, but it was not completed until after the war, in 1950.

The Niemelä croft is like an organic part of the landscape. It consists of over fifteen log buildings, each of which has a grey patina. The buildings were moved in 1909 from Konginkangas to the Seurasaari Open Air Museum in Helsinki.

and top level technology with a life lived close to nature. Many families own a holiday home in the countryside. Finland is a country of modern design and architecture, where virtually every home has some everyday design objects. Here in Finland we drink more coffee than anywhere else in the world – often from mugs featuring illustrations of the adventures of the Moomins, the fairy-tale characters created by artist Tove Jansson. The Moomins are nowadays loved all over the world, but the Finns also have a special attachment to the Moomin house. Sometimes it seems many people in Finland would actually want to live in a Moomin house, though Finns also appreciate modern architecture and there seems to be an increased interest in architect-designed individual houses.

FROM PEAT HUT TO URBANISATION
The journey from the ancient Finnish conical peat-covered hut and chimneyless cottage to a single-family house with all modern comforts and a domestic life dominated by entertainment and information technology is very long. Nevertheless, in today's modern dwelling one can still find parallels with the past. The modern Finns of the 2010s still value living peacefully close to nature, and doing chores in their own yard or garden. They also appreciate interiors with wooden surfaces, taking a sauna and sitting in front of a blazing fire. Popular in single-family houses since the 1970s has been a combined kitchen-dining-living space, which forms the centre of home life, and where the family busy themselves by the kitchen stove – almost like in the ancient Finnish conical hut or the typical main room of a traditional farmhouse. The modern version inevitably also includes a television.

The roots of the Finnish home stretch both in practice and in the Finnish language to the word "kota" (hut). For thousands of years following the last Ice Age that covered the area of present-day Finland, the people lived mostly next to water, and got by with fishing and hunting. On the

 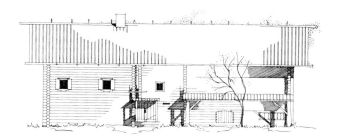

The traditional Karelian house was divided into two parts. The family lived upstairs at one end, while their animals were kept downstairs at the opposite end. The Pertinotša house, which represents the north Russian style and was built in the 19th century, was moved from Suojärvi to Seurasaari in 1939.

basis of scarce archaeological finds, it has been possible to make some assumptions about the multi-skilled tribes and their various fixed and temporary dwellings. More permanent huts were assembled from wooden poles covered with animal skins, birch bark and peat. The fireplace was placed either in the centre of the hut or outside where most of the domestic chores were carried out. During the summer, people also lived in a mobile hut built from wooden poles. By the late Stone Age, the corner jointing technique for log construction, forming a rectangular frame for the peat hut, was already known in the territory of Finland. Also at that time people built interconnected "row houses" consisting of large rectangular peat huts.[2]

The technique of constructing log cabins with a centrally placed stove spread to Finland from the east from around the 4th century. As agriculture became established as the main livelihood and habitation became permanent during the 10th century, tall single-room chimneyless cabins became more common. The walls of the chimneyless cabin were constructed from unhewn round logs, and in the corner nearest the door, on top of a log frame, was a chimneyless oven built in stone. The smoke was let out of the cabin through small hatches made from hewn planks, and these also provided some daylight in the sooty and dark interior. Later on, the floor plan of large log cabins was based on the principle of a long and evenly wide symmetrical two-room cottage that could be extended lengthways, while smaller cabins consisted of a main room together with an entrance porch and one or more additional small rooms. Several outbuildings were built in the vicinity of the house, such as a sauna, threshing barn, animal barn and storage buildings. Ovens and stoves with chimneys as well as glass-paned windows became common in wealthier farmhouses from the 18th century onwards. The exteriors of the log buildings, both in the countryside and in the towns, were not given any surface treatments and so the wood simply turned grey. The practice of painting facades with red ochre paint began to spread from the late 18th century onwards, first in the cities and later slowly in the countryside. Also around the same time began the practice of cladding log facades with boarding, again first the wealthiest urban houses and later the rural houses.[3]

Almost everything at that time was built from wood: from churches and townhouses, handsome rural manor houses and large peasant houses to small-holding crofter's cottages and landless crofters' huts, as well as carriages, furniture and utility objects. Log houses were easy to construct, extend and even relocate. Their durability was increased by the fact that water was not used abundantly inside the houses; for bathing and washing purposes, there was, both in the countryside and in the cities, a separate sauna building at the rear of the yard.

The roots of the lifestyle in a modern Finnish single-family house can be found not only in the rural areas but also in the towns, where the houses were until the late 19th century built like small farmhouses. With their own livestock and kitchen gardens, the people living in the areas of wooden houses in the cities lived a fairly self-reliant life. In addition to the low, mostly log-construction houses, built following the street line, each plot included a number of utility buildings and sheds. Any remaining plot boundaries were marked with wooden fences.

Finnish cities changed with industrialization during the second half of the 19th century, when a large number of people moved from the countryside to work in the newly established factories. The working class areas of the larger cityes were built with tenement blocks comprised of small lodgings. However, some of the workers with traditional building skills built for themselves, often without the use of any real plans, their own cottage or shack in areas of self-build properties at the outskirts of the city. The houses were placed in a somewhat arbitrary manner. The small, often only single-room cottage was later extended, as finances permitted.[4] A well-known example of such a working class community that emerged spontaneously without any master plan is the Pispala district in Tampere.

The standard and types of housing varied greatly between the different social classes across Europe during the early 20th century. Finland was still at that time an autonomous grand duchy of Russia, and one of Europe's poorest and most agrarian countries. One hundred years ago, in certain remote areas of eastern Finland people were still living in chimneyless cottages, while at the same time the most recent houses in Helsinki for the bourgeoisie had lifts, electricity, running water, bathtubs and telephones. Meanwhile, the factory workers in the vicinity of the bourgeoisie lived in cramped conditions with no amenities, and usually with the whole family, sometimes two families, living in one room, often with a relative from the countryside or a family friend as a tenant. In addition, a large part of the population were the so-called parasites or vagrants, who, with no home of their own, were forced to spend the night in the corner of other people's homes.

Finland proclaimed independence in December 1917, but turbulence from the Russian

Herman Gesellius, Armas Lindgren and Eliel Saarinen had Hvitträsk, in Kirkkonummi, built in 1901-1903 as a home for their families as well as a joint architects office. Motifs from Finnish mediaeval churches can be seen in the Jugendstil fireplace corner of the dining room of the Saarinen family's home.

Revolution and, above all, a sharp division in livelihood opportunities and living conditions pushed the country already at the beginning of the following year into civil war. This had long-lasting effects on the Finnish people and society.

THE HISTORY OF THE FINNISH SINGLE-FAMILY HOUSE LIFESTYLE

In the class society of one hundred years ago the gap in the quality of life between the owners of manor houses and the destitute occupants of the landless crofter's hut was huge. Nowadays, in the far more egalitarian Finland, in terms of official statistical categories the old aristocratic family mansion, the farmhouse, and the small transportable cabin all come under the same large category, namely the "single-family house", even though strictly speaking they are not representatives of such a typology at all.

The single-family house is conceptually a relatively new phenomenon, the origins of which in Finland are linked to modern industrialization and urbanization and the subsequent efforts to improve the conditions of the working class. With the rapid industrialization during the 19th century a large amount of the rural population in Europe moved to the city, which led to overcrowding and poverty among the working population as well as the spread of disease. It was to alleviate this increasingly worsening problem that the garden city ideology, developed by Ebenezer Howard in England in the late 1890s, first came about, with the desire to combine the best of rural and urban lifestyles. The garden city idea spread to Finland in the late 19th century and was first taken up as an ideal by the upper classes, and only later as an ideal way of living for the working class. Villa areas designed by archi-

Oiva Kallio received fifth prize in the Brändö Villastad villa competition in 1908 for his Jugendstil proposal with German-Austrian influences. The Kulosaari villa district designed by Lars Sonck had been founded the previous year.

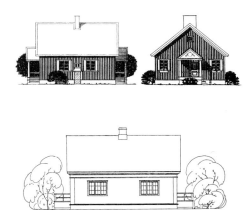

The City of Helsinki Social Welfare Board standardised design for a house for two working class families was based on a competition proposal by Kauno and Oiva Kallio from 1914 (above). Elias and Martti Paalanen's standardised house for two families, from 1921, for the Ministry of Social Affairs (below).

tects for wealthy people began to be built outside the urban centres in the early 20th century. A number of villa communities were established near Helsinki, such as Kulosaari, Kauniainen and Haaga. Architects drew up the town plans for the areas and designed the individual villas. In this context, a "villa" meant mostly a large architect-designed single-family house but also a summer residence commissioned by bourgeois and upper middle class families. The designation in Finnish "omakotitalo" ("one's own house" or literally "own home house"), essentially a detached house, originally referred to working class and middle class housing, often "pattern book" standardized houses placed on small rented plots. Decades later, the borders of the definitions became blurred, as the size of villas was reduced while that of single-family houses increased, and class distinctions evened out. Eventually, the single-family house was accepted as a generally applicable concept.[5]

The principle behind the single-family house ideology was to improve workers' living conditions. There was a desire to house workers in a home of their own, though not necessarily in a house of their own. The house located on a small plot suitable for cultivating a kitchen garden was considered, however, to be the best form of dwelling, and which would increase the working class's sense of belonging and patriotism. Two distinct groups spoke for placing the working class population in their own houses: representatives of the working class who wanted to alleviate the cramped and miserable living conditions, and representatives of the bourgeoisie who believed they could eradicate communism and anarchy and suppress the class struggle by making available to the proletariat houses that they could call their own, and situated on their own patches of land. One of the first projects of this kind was started in the Helsinki parish of Malmi-Tapanila, where in 1906 a private company founded a garden city on land they had bought adjacent to the railway line, and began to sell to townspeople who were suffering from the misery of the housing provision small plots, and which they would pay for in instalments. In addition to self-build schemes, also two-storey pattern book-type houses, each intended for two working class families, were constructed for sale, and also payable in instalments.[6]

The cities of Tampere, Kotka, and Viipuri began already in the 1910s to build the first working class residential areas. Elsewhere in Finland, however, the municipalities did not begin construction until the 1920s, that is, after independence and the civil war, when social responsibility began to increase and the ideology of single-family houses made its final breakthrough. Also factories set up housing areas for their workers. Apart from elsewhere in Europe, influences also came from the USA, where large working class housing areas and mass-produced, inexpensive standardised houses were being built. In Finland architects designed for both cities and industrial communities working class housing areas as well as different dwelling types, ranging from single-family houses to houses accommodating several families. The housing areas became uniform because one of the conditions for funding was compliance to approved standardised drawings. Architects designed standardised houses for both specific regions and nationwide use.[7]

THE DWELLING IDEALS OF FUNCTIONALISM

In the late 1920s a new philosophy and style arrived in Finland from central Europe, namely functionalism. Its ideals included social equality but also the objective to build large numbers of so-called "existence minimum" houses, which would be cheap, filled with natural light, hygienic and with a layout that was as universal and practical as possible. Cities had to be planned with clear zonal distinctions between different functions, placing jobs and some services in their own designated zones and placing housing separately in green and healthy suburban zones. At that time, people could not imagine that such an urban design model based on the use of the private car would later generate major traffic problems. The ideology of functionalism quickly spread around the world. Its universal form ideals initially favoured flat roofs and white houses with smooth-faced facades and interiors, and individual motifs

Alvar and Aino Aalto's home in Munkkiniemi, Helsinki, was completed in 1936. The house functioned also for a long time as their architects' office, which was separated from the living room by a sliding door. The authentic atmosphere in the comfortable living room has been retained over the decades. Aalto's second wife, Elissa, lived in the house until her death in 1994.

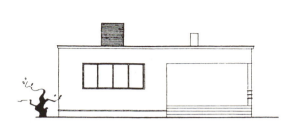

A functionalist-style 58 m² standardised house with a mono-pitched roof, designed by Elias Paalanen. The house was published in a Ministry of Social Affairs leaflet in 1935.

Väinö Vähäkallio designed the Kaukopää pulp mill, which began operating in 1935, and adjacent residential area. The works manager lived in the impressive functionalist-style house.

The grand and luxurious Villa Mairea, in Noormarkku, Pori, built in 1939 for Harry and Maire Gullichsen, the director of the Ahlström company and his wife, is one of the world's best known private homes. Alvar and Aino Aalto designed the Gesamtkunstwerk down to the smallest details, refining the ideas that first emerged when designing their own home.

The 1940 sales catalogue of the Puutalo company exudes the optimism of the interim peace period. The factory-produced Päivölä standardised house was designed by Jorma Järvi and Erik Lindroos.

Standardised houses A2 and A21, from 1941, for the settlement committee of the Central Union of the Agricultural Society.

such as ribbon windows, as well as round windows and steel railings familiar from ships.

Stylistically, pure functionalism remained rather uncommon in Finnish single-family houses until the second half of the 1930s, and was mainly a phenomenon favoured by younger architects and their wealthy clients who followed the trends of the time. Many single-family houses in the cities and rural villages were still built in the style of the previous decades, flavoured with the form language of late Jugendstil art nouveau and classicism, although they began to be increasingly combined with features of functionalism. In the 1930s the Finnish state published collections of standardised drawings, and functionalist inspired standardised house models included in these began to appear in areas of single-family houses across the country.

The house Alvar and Aino Aalto designed and had built for their own family in Munkkiniemi, Helsinki, in 1936, as well as Villa Mairea, near Pori, completed in 1939, the large and luxurious home for the Ahlström company director's family, where they would entertain guests, are internationally well-known examples of functionalist architecture from that period. However, the style and design of these two houses are very far from the typical Finnish small single-family house of the time.

THE YEARS OF ECONOMIC DEPRESSION IN HOUSING

The biggest construction project in Finland's history is the reconstruction that followed after the Winter War of 1939–1940 and the Continuation War and Lapland War of 1941–1945. This entailed building houses for the relocated Finnish population that had been forced to leave their homes which were now on the Soviet side of the newly drawn border between Finland and the Soviet Union. The rebuilding process continued until the 1950s. A

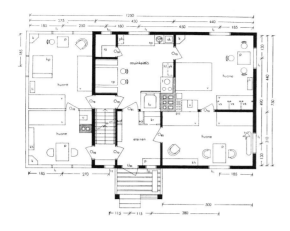 

The extendable single-family standardised house MKL 6, from 1943, for the Central Union of the Agricultural Society, designed by Aarne Hytönen, Yrjö Lindegrén and Olli Pöyry from the Finnish Association of Architects Reconstruction Bureau. Standardised houses were designed by the country's leading architects.

huge number of dwellings was needed quickly just for the almost 500 000 refugees that were evacuated from the areas – Karelia, Salla, Kuusamo and Petsamo – that were annexed to the Soviet Union. In addition, thousands of homes had been destroyed in Soviet air bombardments and the Germans retreating from Lapland had destroyed most of the buildings in the province.

The Everyman's Building Guide [Jokamiehen rakennusopas] from 1946, aimed at the "low income builder", described the war-induced housing shortage faced by hundreds of thousands of people: "We face a reconstruction task that is extraordinarily extensive. --- Countless war widows, disabled and relocated families with their many children are without a roof over their heads. They are scattered all over our country". The aim of the guide book was optimistically to encourage people to build both single-family houses and to voluntarily offer help in other people's building projects: "There is no better deed than the comrades-in-arms honouring the memory of a fallen soldier by building his widow and orphans a home where they have protection against the autumn rain and winter frost." The Everyman's Building Guide presented a variety of standardised construction drawings, comprehensive advice for building log and plank construction houses, relying on a tried and tested tradition – most of which also even today would prove useful. At that time most of the population still lived in the countryside. Hence the book provided guidance for building a baking oven and suggested reserving a place in the home for a loom and carpenter's bench. The importance of kitchen design was highlighted by describing the everyday life: "We know that the mistress of the house is the first one in the morning to begin the working day and the last one to finish it in the evening."[8]

The uniform street view of a single-family housing area in Pieksämäki from the post-war reconstruction period. The simple forms of the houses are an expression of the archetypal house.

A standardised house, 2.02k, designed by Alvar Aalto for the A. Ahlström company sales catalogue during the 1940s. The rare type fulfilled the requirements of a more luxurious villa.

During the war years and afterwards until the early 1960s, one and a half storey pitched-roofed wooden houses with high plinths became common throughout Finland. Even though as a result of the war many single-parent families and new family groupings had been created, the standardised houses were designed according to the ideals of the time period, that is, the nuclear family. The houses had the same type of often almost square floor plan, where the rooms were placed around the fireplaces in the centre of the building. On the ground floor were usually a kitchen, a living room and a bedroom. Funds permitting, it was possible to build two rooms upstairs for the use of the family or for renting out. A single chimney flue made the house energy efficient and saved on building costs, although it led to a similarity in the floor plan solutions.[9]

In the first half of the 1940s houses were often constructed with a log frame, but at the same time the so-called balloon frame construction, which saved on the amount of wood needed, became more common and eventually overtook log construction. Some of the houses were assembled from prefabricated wooden elements. The standardised houses from the post-war reconstruction era had, in the spirit of functionalism, a simplified appearance. They were, in fact, a continuation of the house models from the previous decades. The similar looking, beautifully simple houses, one and a half storeys high, with harmonious proportions, had already been built in the 1930s and the roots of this rational type of house can be found already in Swedish 18th century drawings for model houses.[10]

The standardised houses of the post-war reconstruction period were mostly designed by architects. In the late 1930s the Finnish Association of Architects began to systematize the dimensions of building construction together with general standardization and rationalization procedures. Along with the post-war reconstruction, the first large-scale application of the reform was evident in the construction of single-family houses. The pur-

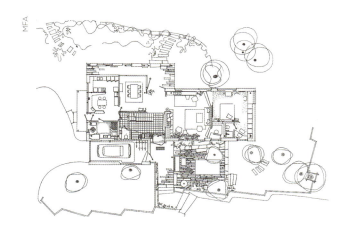

Aarne Ervi and his first wife Inkeri pose for a photo in the stylish living room of their home, Villa Ervi, in the mid-1950s. The villa in Kuusisaari, Helsinki, completed in 1950, was presented in popular magazines and became a model for the dream single-family home. Designer furniture, lamps, hardwood cupboards, leopard and zebra hides, and an attractive garden together formed a unique Gesamtkunstwerk. The influences from Aalto's Villa Mairea can be seen in the series of open spaces on the ground floor as well as in the details. First floor plan is on the left.

pose of standardization was to improve the quality of the houses, to make them more aesthetically appealing and, above all, to reduce construction costs, so that everyone could obtain a decent dwelling. Following the reconstruction after the Winter War, several expert bodies, including the Finnish Association of Architects' Post-War Reconstruction Bureau, developed drawings of standardised house designs. A large number of universally applicable model drawings were produced for single-family houses and utility buildings, as well as their construction, components, fireplaces and fixed furniture, in particular kitchen cupboards. The drawings were printed for distribution as the so-called "Finnish building information file".[11]

Planning was often done as voluntary work in the evenings, and the authorities in charge of reconstruction distributed the drawings to builders free of charge or for a minimal fee. Houses were built in both the countryside and the cities to a large extent as self-build schemes, often using volunteers. However, compliance with the drawings became a condition for securing a loan. Master plans were drawn up for the housing areas, where different house types were placed in their separate groups. Construction was supervised and directed both on each individual site and in the overall areas, which throughout the country became very uniform.[12]

There seems to have been an unspoken consensus about the appearance of the standardised houses of the post-war reconstruction period, as shown by their uniformity, as they spread throughout the country, in the cities and the countryside, and even to the remotest villages. Today the areas of single-family houses from the reconstruction period are verdant, comfortable and highly valued. Despite the uniformity, there is no monotony, but rather the areas are harmonious and a suitable amount of difference can be seen in the colouring, details, fences and yard vegetation – even between completely identical standardised houses.

With the advent of extensive, standardised house construction, people's standard of living improved considerably, and in the 1940s and 1950s similar looking single-family houses spread throughout Finland. Particularly in the countryside, however, the majority of the houses were situated on plots with no communal water supply or plumbing; the toilet, sauna and firewood storage were located in outbuildings. In the beginning of the 1950s, two-thirds of Finns lived in the countryside or sparsely populated areas, and many houses were still outside the reach of the electricity supply network.

Life during the 1940s and 1950s in Finland, as in other war torn countries, was marked by material shortages. The plots of single-family houses in the city had space for vegetable gardens and also livestock could be kept to supplement people's own food production. Meals were still prepared in many homes on a wood-heated stove and houses with bathrooms were rare. Due to the housing shortage, it was customary to rent out one of the rooms to a lodger, and in many one and a half storey single-family houses the upper part was turned into a separate rental dwelling. Leisure time was scarce, though going to the cinema was a popular activity. In addition to the small-number of newspapers and magazines, culture was also brought into Finnish homes with the radio, though with just one channel operating for a few hours each day almost the entire nation listened to the same programmes. Despite large social differences, people in Finland lived in an era with a homogenous culture.

There is a lot of nostalgia associated with the standardised houses from the post-war reconstruction era. This probably has to do with the fact that so many Finns have fond first-hand memories of their own childhood home, or their grandmother's home. People living under the stress and hurry of contemporary life can easily endorse childhood nostalgia by acquiring a house, furniture and tableware that remind them of their childhood, and that need is also recognised and appealed to in commercial marketing. The standardised houses from the post-war reconstruction era have become almost icons for the Finnish home.

THE ARMS RACE OF MODERN HOMES

Finnish society was rapidly industrialized, urbanized and modernised during the 1960s and 1970s. Mass migration emptied the countryside and the population became concentrated in cities, where thousands of new apartment buildings were built from prefabricated concrete elements. Also, many single-family houses were built with the help of government subsidized low-interest loans, often with the people carrying out a large part of the construction work themselves. From the 1950s onwards, architects designed terraced houses and so-called linked houses, which became new popular forms of dwelling.

During the second half of the 1950s, a type of international-inspired modernism became the predominant style of architecture. Right angles were favoured, as were horizontal lines,

The aluminium and glass single-family house designed by Aulis Blomstedt for a Canadian competition in 1954 was ahead of its time. Architects who had studied under Blomstedt designed houses following this model during the 1960s and 1970s.

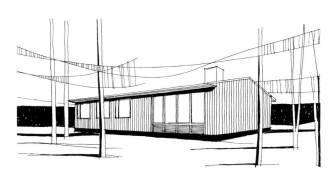

Reino Lammin-Soila's modern standardised house, 97 m² in area plus a cellar, was the result of a competition held in 1956 organised by the Finnish state's Communications Unit and the Ministry of Labour's housing research committee.

strip windows and carefully considered simple streamlined design. Single-family houses were mostly single storey, and floor plans were developed to be as functional and spacious as possible. The feeling of space was enhanced by sliding doors and large, often wall-to-wall, windows that aimed to integrate the dwelling with the surrounding nature. The roofs of the single-family houses were changed, first to slightly sloping pitched roofs and mono-pitched roofs and later to flat roofs. The tall foundation plinths and ventilated space below the raised ground floor were replaced by a slab foundation resting directly on the ground and plinths that were as low as possible.

The 1957 publication *The Everyman as a Builder [Jokamies rakentajana]* indicated that new trends were already evident. On the basis of fire safety, the book recommended building only single-storey detached houses, but which, when necessary, could also include a basement. The one and a half storey house was condemned because "it does not follow contemporary trends in tastes", but is a "blatant, sharp, linear structure defying the winds".[13]

The houses of the poverty stricken post-war reconstruction period were regarded as hopelessly out of fashion, and people wanted to make a clear break with them. *The Home Book [Omakotikirja]*, a guide book published in 1960 and edited by four architects, which gave advice for people wanting to construct a house for their own family, bluntly described the standardised house from the post-war reconstruction era, as "an ugly straggler that does not adapt to the Finnish landscape." In *The Home Book* all one and a half storey houses were judged as clumsy, unsuccessful in terms of their proportions, uneconomical, and their attic spaces unpleasant. As good examples, the book presented new low houses with large windows and shallow sloping roofs as well as unique luxurious detached houses.[14] Such houses had then recently been built in Tapiola garden city in Espoo. Tapiola became the

An atrium house in a minimalist style designed by Toivo Korhonen for his family in Lauttasaari, Helsinki, completed in 1960.

The house designed by Aarne Ervi for Heikki von Hertzen, chairman of the Housing Foundation, built in Tapiola in 1962, followed the modernist ideals of the time.

The glass-fibre-reinforced plastic Futuro House, designed by Matti Suuronen, with a space-age-style interior décor, became an international, if short-lived, success. The serial production of the Futuro House began in 1968, but ended in 1973 with the oil crisis. The small alcove kitchen can be seen in the background in this American marketing photograph.

progressive trendsetter in Finnish housing and architecture, indeed a national source of pride, and also it also received a great deal of international attention.

New ideals in housing were clearly visible in the book *Living Close to Nature*, from 1966, which introduced the best of the single-family house architecture of the period, many of them from Tapiola. When looking at the houses featured in the book, one notices that Finland had already recovered from the war and that the standard of living was rising rapidly. Private cars were beginning to become more common and architects were designing unique, elegant houses in the suburbs, which ironically were being called dormer suburbs. The largest and most luxurious houses in the book are reminiscent of the millionaire villas in the USA from the 1950s, with their stylishly minimalist interiors and large immaculate lawns. The largest houses in the book had two garages, two bathrooms, a swimming pool and sauna and in connection with the kitchen a separate entrance and room for a housemaid.[15]

The book *We Live in Our Own House* [*Asumme omassa talossa*], from 1969, presented mainly standardised and prefabricated houses suitable for ordinary families. A typical prefabricated house of that time was one storey with a rectangular or L-shaped floor plan, with a timber-framed construction that was clad in red brick, and with a very shallow pitched or monopitched roof. The book also featured a number of individually designed houses, as well as the architects' own houses, noting in one case that "swimming pools are nowadays being built a lot, and one could even consider it a craze". A house designed by Viljo Revell, completed in 1962, had a "double living room" because "the design was based on a working housewife's desire for a kitchen where she would not feel isolated".[16]

With the slender wooden prefabricated element Moduli 225 system, designed by Kristian Gullichsen and Juhani Pallasmaa, from 1968, it was possible to quickly erect buildings with different floor plans. In the 1960s and 1970s several similar prefabricated housing systems with slender structures, flat roofs and non-existent eaves came on the market, but they all failed to meet the demands of the severe Finnish climate conditions.

The rapid change in the standard of living can be seen in the single-family houses from the late 1950s onwards. Separate saunas in the yard, outdoor toilets and sheds represented a past era of material shortages. Now the houses had modern indoor comforts, such as a built-in WC, bathroom and sauna preferably with an electric-heated stove, rather than the traditional wood-heated stove. Novelties of the time in the single-family house included a utility room and cold room. Open kitchens and galley kitchens were fashionable. The life of the mother became easier when home appliances appeared on the market, and ordinary wage earners could save up to purchase a refrigerator, washing machine, vacuum cleaner and telephone. Another popular phenomenon of the period was the hobby room, the idea of which was to bring together the nuclear family in common leisure activities. This room soon fell out of use, however, because when television became widespread it revolutionized not only how families spent their time but also how the living room was furnished. The father often got, nevertheless, his own "hobby space", because at the time when most families purchased a car it also became common to build a heated garage at the end of the new detached house.

The Finnish home decoration ideals of the 1960s included clean-lined open fireplaces, understated modern sofa groups, hardwood veneer-surfaced furniture and built-in cupboards, as well as walls painted with strong colour effects. Also, one of the walls of the living room could be left with an exposed brick surface.

At the end of the decade arrived bright interior colours, chipboard furniture with foam rubber cushions, plastic furniture and lamps as well as the large patterned printed fabrics made by Marimekko. During the 1960s there was still only a limited amount of imported goods available in stores, and so for furnishing and household articles the use of international award-winning Finnish design and curtain fabrics were favoured. These stylistic ideals were so clear and consistent that they were passed on in one way or another to the whole population. Class differences had begun to stabilize, Finnish culture was still homogeneous and the whole nation watched the same television programmes and commercials. Indeed, it is through advertisements that one can find an explanation for many of the phenomena that passed through society as a whole. Those old enough would still remember the TV commercial from the 1960s and 1970s claiming "a happy family lives in a brick house".

Exemplary models and dreams of modern single-family homes, interiors and gardens were spread throughout Finland in the 1960s in the few above-mentioned books that discussed these topics, but, above all, in interior design and women's magazines. The magazine *Kaunis Koti* [Beautiful Home], first published in 1948, was for almost two decades the only interior decoration magazine in Finland that had a more didactic approach, targeted at the upper social classes, where designers and architects were influential. In 1971 the magazine merged with another magazine *Avotakka* [Open Fireplace], which since its

Matti Suuronen's Venturo House CF-45 was presented to the international media in 1971. Different sized single-family houses and other buildings could be assembled from large glass-fibre-reinforced plastic elements. Production was started in several countries before the 1973 oil crisis brought it to a halt.

first year of publication, 1967, had been pursuing a broader readership, presenting celebrities' homes and single-family houses. Later the number of Finnish interior magazines soared to almost tenfold, and newspapers began to publish interior design ideas.

In the 1960s and following decades, Finnish society underwent reform and became pluralistic in many ways. For example, there was increasing public discussion about the struggle for equality between men and women and the sharing of domestic work, which then became reflected in home life. There was a shift to a consumer society, the self-sufficiency of families was reduced and almost everything that was necessary – and even unnecessary – could be readily purchased in shops. The start of the domestic arms race in washing machines, freezers, coffeemakers, colour TVs,

Romanticism is a common feature in present day single-family houses. One of the many exemplars has been the Moominhouse at the Moomin World theme park in Naantali, and which was realised on the basis of the drawings and books by Tove Jansson.

toasters, liquidizers, humidifiers, dishwashers, hairdryers, stereos, egg cookers, bread machines, video recorders, microwaves, and currently computers dates from those decades. Finnish homes became filled with commodities. Growing food for home needs was no longer necessary, so the kitchen gardens of the single-family houses became decorative gardens, the flat lawn of which was cut regularly with a mower and watered regularly with a sprinkler. In recent years, the house owners have been targeted in the marketing of lawn tractors, outdoor jacuzzis, gas-fired barbecues, patio heaters, and wine cellars. The living standard of the average Finnish resident of a single-family house has really changed in the last half century.

Living in a single-family house has traditionally been associated with the perception of an ideal nuclear family. The independent nuclear family is, in fact, a fairly late phenomenon, because still in the early 20th century communal living was common in the rural areas, where many families and generations, as well as maids and hired hands, all lived in the same house. Dying at an early age was not uncommon, and so stepfamilies that had been formed as a result of widowhood were common. The ideal of a father, mother and two children in a nuclear family is only a later, modern-day phenomenon, and nowadays only partly corresponds to the reality of the Finnish way of life. Today, about half of marriages end in divorce, single-parent and stepfamilies are common, and the concept of a family also fits the idea of, say, two women and a child or two men forming a family. At the same time, the number of people living alone has already increased to one-third of the population.

Previously, among the upper social classes the home was, due to a person's career and social status, regarded as a place that demonstrated status and where guests would be received. In the countryside and among the urban working class, in turn, it was very normal for neighbours and friends to stop by unannounced. This was the time before telephones, and the sense of community was stronger than it is today. The bourgeois life associated with homes for entertaining important guests has become rare, and instead the home has become a very private place, where generally only the closest family and friends are invited. Visiting people at their home has become more formal, as the visits are agreed in advance, and instead of informally offering a cup of coffee and a bun, three-course dinners with wine are becoming more popular, just as in the bourgeois homes during the early 20th century.

FROM BOXES TO MOOMIN HOUSES

Architectural styles and housing trends have fluctuated greatly in recent decades. I remember from my childhood in the early 1970s an article in the magazine *Avotakka* in which a one and a half storey house from the post-war reconstruction period was transformed into a flat-roofed house by demolishing the upper floor and constructing in its place a roof with wide eaves. The radical and expensive alterations carried out for reasons of appearance were surprising to me because our family had earlier lived in a cosy one and a half storey single-family house. Certainly, the flat roofed detached houses with large windows presented in the journals at that time represented the finest type of living that I knew of, and my own family, too, lived in a modern terraced house decorated in bright colours.

The general stylistic ideals soon changed again. Just when the dream of a modern house with large windows had permeated all of Finland, the international energy crisis of 1973 forced people again to reduce the size of the windows in accordance with the revised building regulations for new houses. At the same time, also the dream of owning a private swimming pool started to sound ridiculous. In later years, many houses changed their flat roof to a pitched or mono-pitched roof. The modern houses of the 1960s and 1970s were functional and full of natural light, but the ideal of rectangular, simplified houses went somewhat too far when also wooden single-family houses were built with a flat roof and without any eaves. Perhaps people also began to long for alternatives, as thousands of houses in the same style, originally intended for urban plots, had risen rapidly all over the country. Low-rise modernist houses were criticized in the media as being unsuitable for traditional rural and village landscapes.

Up until the 1960s and 1970s, standard-

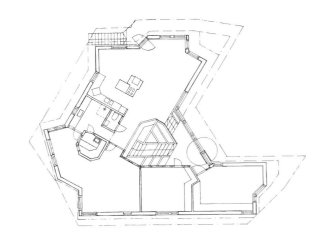

The single-family house in Helsinki designed by Raili and Reima Pietilä in the 1980s has a polymorphous floor plan.

ised and prefabricated houses were primarily designed by architects, but in the 1980s their design and development shifted to the technical teams working at prefabricated housing factories and to anonymous designers. Single-family houses became consumer products, and as such influenced by advertising and media-generated ideals.[17] House manufacturers began offering the consumers models which combined the floor plans of modern houses from previous years with historicising and romantic influences. Steep roofed "cuckoo clock" houses were created, as were houses with mansard roofs, and textured bricks and arches both in the interior and exterior, as familiar from the Mediterranean package tour holiday resorts. Large windows were divided into panes by placing fake mullions on top of the glass. In the 1990s house designs became popular which imitated the early 20th century villas, vicarages and country manor houses. Over the years, Finnish house building splintered into a diverse spectrum of mostly retro-style prefabricated houses. It was argued that the inspiration for romantic houses was taken from dreams of manor house lifestyles and from television series. The manufacturers of the prefabricated houses defended their actions by saying they were producing houses that ordinary consumers wanted.

Olli Lehtovuori, chief architect of the Housing Board, did not mince his words in his book *The Well-Designed Small House [Hyvin suunniteltu pientalo]*, published in 1984: "The strength of advertising and the diversity of options easily confuse the person looking for a

Villa Nötterkulla, in Inkoo, from 1990, designed by Georg Grotenfelt, carries the spirit of Aalto's Villa Mairea.

Villa Lilius-Ohlström, in Padasjoki, designed by Georg Grotenfelt at the beginning of the 1980s. Wood is an appropriate material for the construction of single-family houses. It is a renewable natural source and binds carbon dioxide.

home. Fashion trends and heavy-handed advertising can make even the most level headed home-buying families throw caution to the wind. --- In Finland the importance of planning has been seriously underestimated In the most basic sense, this is manifested in self-build. Many builder families believe that the design should not cost anything."[18]

Tore Tallqvist summed up the change in an essay in the book *Finnish House*, from 1986:

A wooden house in Vantaa, designed by Anna Puisto and Marcel Ulmer, completed in 2004, includes a steel balcony the width of the whole façade, together with sliding sun louvers.

"A topical design problem of the single-family house is the gap between the preconceptions of architects and users. There are no consistent and uniform definitions of good architecture for single-family houses." He compounded this distinction by placing side by side pictures of a modern flat-roofed and eavesless wooden summer cottage from the 1960s, designed by radical young architects Kirmo Mikkola and Juhani Pallasmaa, and the Moomin house. "Neither example is a typical single-family house, but they constitute a frame of reference for the architecture of today's single-family house", and they "also show the conflict between an architect's and a layman's way of thinking."[19]

THE FINNISH IDEAL OF A HOME OF ONE'S OWN

Finns have rapidly become urbanized, and the tradition of living in urban high-rise apartment blocks is short. The dream dwelling for many people is still one in a rural-like setting: a single-family house in the vicinity of a forest and situated by the water's edge, yet close to the amenities of the city. Annually around 11 000–15 000 new single-family houses are built in Finland. Finland has currently about one million single-family houses, about 300 000 terraced houses and about one million apartments.

The viewpoint that life in a single-family house is superior to other lifestyles has been justified in interview-based studies in terms of, for instance, freedom, independence, individuality, closeness to nature, finding one's own peace, social distance from the neighbours, the ability to influence one's own living environment and obtaining something meaningful to do. These justifications may be seen as contradictory with the fact that the majority of single-family houses constructed in Finland are almost identical-looking traditional standardised houses, readily ordered from the catalogues of prefabricated house manufacturers, and situated next to each other on small plots of land. According to researchers, this conflict between perceptions and reality can be explained by the fact that a large part of

Sairanen House in Helsinki, designed by Jan Söderlund and Tuulikki Raivio in the early 2000s, opens directly towards the south and the sunlight.

the homebuilders' wishes and desires are not very independent. On the contrary, they seek the same as everyone else. On the other hand, there is a minority of homebuilders, those with the highest incomes, who seek to differentiate themselves from others by building individualistic houses. The construction of single-family houses has been associated with tradition and continuity as well as people striving for a better life. With regard to tradition, it is a matter of idealized images, of the human desire to relive moments of happiness from one's own childhood home. Both living in a single-family house and its construction have been associated with many cultural-related general beliefs. The historical and cultural developments of Finnish society have shaped the national identity, which is strongly based on the ownership of a house and the surrounding land. The acquisition of a house of one's own is the culmination of this kind of thinking, and even a national ideal.[20]

NOSTALGIA AND ROMANTICISM

Modernist single-family houses, usually designed by architects, were a mainstream phenomenon throughout the whole of Finland from the 1940s until the 1970s. By comparison, the modernist style single-family house has not had a similar position in, for example, the United States, where it seems that over the decades the most popular choice has been historical retro-style houses.

It is believed that the popularity of traditional style houses, which resemble old houses, is related to the fact that they represent a story of the return home, a return to the time and place of innocence before the present modern world. The traditional style symbolizes the fantasy of a safe, family-centred time long ago in the past.[21]

The popularity of new houses built in a historical nostalgic style seems to have increased in recent times, and there is a similar phenomenon occurring in several other countries. Today, the best-selling models from the Finnish prefabricated house manufacturers are the single-family houses that imitate the mansions and romantic villas of bygone times. In fact, modern house designs barely even exist in the manufacturers' catalogues.

Most of the single-family houses currently built in Finland are designed and fabricated by manufacturers as "house packages", that is, as prefabricated units. Prefabricated houses can be made just as durable as those built on site, but a wider variety of options should exist parallel with the traditional models, that is, architecturally high-quality prefabricated houses that would be simple and timeless, functional, durable and affordable. In recent years, however, there have been signs of consumers' awakening interest in houses representing a modern design language.[22]

Today, only a few percent of the single-family houses built in Finland annually are designed by an architect. Individual architect designed houses are considered expensive, but they can also be cheaper than prefabricated house manufacturers' models. It is also possible to have an individually designed house built by one of the prefabricated house manufacturers. The available prefabrication methods include small elements, large elements and spatial elements, platform construction and the pre-cut system, all of which are also suitable for the construction of individually designed houses.

THE BIGGEST BUILDING PROJECT OF ONE'S LIFE
Many houses are for their owners probably a dream come true, but hardly for all of them. Building one's own home, with all the stages it involves, is a demanding and time-consuming project. It is usually the most expensive investment in a person's life. And all the components should be put together to form a durable, functional and beautiful whole. The journey from the dreams and visions to the completed house brings many new and unexpected things for those getting involved in their first and probably only building project, and construction projects always involve some risks. Although relatively small, the single-family house project is nevertheless a challenge. Many things can go wrong, and so trying to save on costs at the wrong moment can become expensive. Fantasy images and information packages related to real construction options are so plentiful that it pays to be sceptical towards them. When brainstorming for the project it is useful to assess realistically the whole process, funding, and the timetable, as well as one's own potential and ability to participate in the construction. Many home builders take on the first house of their life without knowing enough about how much work, time and expertise in many different fields the project requires. So it is useful first to find out from the relevant guide books what the construction project actually involves.

The safest route for the house builder is to trust professional designers and builders, because it is the only way to get the best result. A skilled architect as the main designer pays back what it costs in designs fees by bringing added value to the construction project when following the client's wishes, and by exceeding expectations through functional solutions, comfortable spaces and the avoidance of wasted floor area. When such architect-designed houses go on the market, they often sell faster and at a higher price than other houses.

When dreaming of life in one's own single-family house, one should keep in mind that there are also those who dream of moving from their single-family house to a terraced house or apartment block with good traffic connections, especially if the children in the family have moved away from home. Living in one's own house requires more than the usual number of domestic chores, such as taking care of the building maintenance and repairs, tending the garden, shovelling snow and organising waste disposal. If one wants carefree living, a terraced house or apartment block is probably the most appropriate dwelling. Architects have developed apartment solutions that go in the direction of the life in a single-family house through the design of courtyard apartments on the ground floor, by making two-storey apartments, by providing apartments with large balconies and by re-

Combining resources to build a number of dwellings can provide high-quality results at an affordable price. Three new houses, grouped together with an existing house, in Hermanni, Helsinki, designed by Marcus Ahlman and Viivi Snellman and completed in 2009. The photo shows the interior of the Ahlman family's terraced house.

serving the rooftops for solutions that function like terraced houses.

HEALTHY AND SICK BUILDINGS

In Finland, just as in other Western countries, there has already for some years been talk about "sick buildings". Research has shown that new building construction techniques and industrial materials, which have become common in many countries since the 1960s, have a significant risk for both internal and external moisture damage. Since the 1960s, the multinational building products industry has continuously been launching on to the market new industrially produced building materials. At the same time, new construction methods have been adopted, though their durability and compatibility have not been tested over time. Thermal insulation in houses received no attention because energy was still cheap. The rapid changes in building from the late 1950s onwards was a consequence of changes in society and the rapid rise in living standards, and this has been seen with similar phenomena in all industrialized countries.

At the latest since the 1990s, it has been noticed that people's health cannot withstand all synthetic building materials, and that wet and leaky structures and moisture damage can in a short time cause chronic respiratory disease and changes at the cellular level of the body. The central challenge in construction as become moisture management. In addition to risky structural solutions, also unnoted construction mistakes as well as poor building site protection cause problems that show up later. Furthermore, the incorrect use of buildings and the neglect of maintenance cause substantial moisture damage.

TOWARDS SUSTAINABLE BUILDING

The construction and use of buildings currently consume more than 40 percent of all energy produced and materials used, and they produce nearly an equal share of both emissions and waste. In response to climate change and environmental catastrophes, Finnish legislation has begun to require increasingly more energy-efficient and low-emission construction. Design is becoming increasingly more demanding, and the biggest changes still lie ahead. Architecture and construction must be based on technical sustainability and energy efficiency.

All buildings should stand on their location as a natural part of the prevailing condi-

Solbranten House, which Bruno Erat designed for his own family, is a true classic of ecological building and energy-saving design. The house, built in Espoo in 1979, has been divided into warm and semi-warm spaces. Solar heat is stored both actively and passively in a vertical container in the middle of the house, from where the warm air is distributed to the rooms. During the cold winters use is made of the fireplace in the middle of the house. There is natural ventilation, together with heat recovery. The grey waters and compostable waste are utilised on the plot and in the conservatory where vegetables are grown. There is a flower meadow growing on the roof.

tions. Within a single country such as Finland, there can be great geographical, climatic and biological differences. Buildings should be intelligently placed as an integral part of their environment and the natural life-cycle by paying attention to the shape of the building and its location on the plot, the utilisation of the climate and sun, the optimal orientation of the windows and necessary shade, as well as the utilisation of natural lighting and ventilation.

If the designer has no control over the natural conditions on the site and is not sufficiently aware of the physics of building, the house can fail: the building envelope wastes energy, moisture problems are created in the structures, the sun overheats the interior spaces and requires the use of mechanical cooling and the heat of the sun cannot even be exploited for the house's energy production.

Integrated natural or combined ventilation systems in buildings are healthy, pleasant for the occupants and affordable. Also the structure of the building should be ventilated in a natural way. For example, enclosed, mechanically ventilated ground floors may be vulnerable to moisture risks if the machinery is not working or its output insufficient. The building is not worth turning into an electricity guzzler, that is, a complex machine, the technical systems of which are extremely vulnerable and which the residents do not know how to use or remember to maintain.

In the planning of the building one should first take advantage of all the natural means available and only then resort to technical devices. The most effective solutions are obvious, technologically simple, and often virtually cost free. Some of them have been in use for centuries, but have later been forgotten. Trusting traditional, well-proven construction materials, techniques and applications is the surest way to a successful solution, but there should also be a parallel development of completely new solutions.

Houses today can be designed to produce renewable energy beyond their own needs. It can be obtained, for instance, through passive solar energy, solar cells and collectors, heat pumps and windmills. Technically and energy-economically sustainable construction means, among other things, an energy-saving form and envelope to the building, energy efficiency and energy self-sufficiency, a long life-cycle, and local and renewable building materials that can be recycled. Because climate change increases rainfall and the frequency of storms, it is of particular importance during both the design phase and construction to address the detailing of the structures and the outer envelope, as well as moisture management and the avoidance of high-risk structures. Carefully designed and constructed houses can last for hundreds of years.

ECO-EFFICIENT LIVING

The placement of dwellings in Finland is increasingly concentrated in a few major population growth centres. Although there is adequate space for construction throughout the country, building spacious single-family housing areas is unecological, expensive and ineffective in terms of services, urban planning and infrastructure, and traffic. Densely built garden cities connected by a rail network, low-rise housing areas with interlinked yards and single-family houses with a floor area of approximately 90–120 m² are the most viable solutions for the suburbs. As building types, terraced houses with two or more storeys are suitable, as are individually designed townhouses, each comprising a single residence, built adjoining one another in rows. These house types enable a dense urban kind of single-family dwelling, with a direct link to a private small garden. Building well-designed, dense low-rise housing can achieve the same land-use efficiency as the dispersed suburban areas comprised of multi-storey apartment blocks. Unnecessary traffic and travel times are reduced when the services, schools and workplaces are within walking and bicycling distance.

Naturally managed green areas secure the survival of animal and plant species and contribute to human well-being. Accordingly, in yards and green areas one should promote "orderly neglect", diversity of nature and species, traditional meadows, pastures, thickets and open ditches. The garden or yard should be allowed to sprawl without care, at least at the edges, where one can also leave decomposable wood and heaps of leaves. Manicured lawns are an ecological vacuum, and their maintenance is costly and wasteful of water. The lush yard, blossoming from spring to autumn, with its traditional nectar-bearing plants and herbs, encourages numerous butterfly species into the area and consequently also attracts birds.

Grey wastewater can be utilised on the plot, and instead of a water-operated toilet one can install a composting or biogas-producing odourless toilet suitable for indoor use. In this way natural eutrophication and water pollution are significantly reduced and nutrients utilised. In the future, all waste should be either recycled or converted into energy.

With eco-efficiency it is possible to achieve a similar standard of living to the current one using only a small proportion of the current energy and material consumption, while still enabling a better quality of life. In the future, people living in a single-family house will be able to save energy while at the same time producing it, without having to worry about waste. In a carefully planned, beautiful-looking house the residents enjoy an abundance of natural light, pleasant natural materials, and natural ventilation that works with gravity. The structures of the house are durable, and living spaces are functional and flexible, depending on living requirements and the seasons. At the height of winter, the core portion of the house is kept warm, and from spring to autumn, the living area of the home extends to the glass verandas heated by the sun. The reused water is used for watering the green house salad crops and the small garden – and flowers, vegetables and herbs grow in the soil produced from the compost. Energy self-sufficiency in the house is taken care of by the sun, a small wind turbine, a heat pump, well-designed easy to use automated technology and the inhabitants of the house who appreciate a comfortable life.

Harri Hautajärvi

FOOTNOTES

1. "The World's Best Countries", A Newsweek study, 2010; European Social Survey (ESS), 2007; "Democracy Barometer 2011", University of Zurich and the Social Science Research Centre Berlin; "Corruption Perception Index 2010", Transparency International; "The Global Gender Gap Report 2010", World Economic Forum; OECD Programme for International Student Assessment (PISA).
2. Huurre 1998, 65–69, 79–88; Muurimäki 2004.
3. Korhonen 1988, 18–47; Latvala.
4. Lampi 2007, 19–26.
5. Saarikangas 1993, 99–111, 167–185; Saarikangas 2004, 14–17; Lampi 2007, 8–9, 19–29; Nurmi 2010, 13–87.
6. Saarikangas 1993, 99–111; Saarikangas 2004, 14–17; Lampi 2007, 28–46.
7. Ibid.
8. Mandelin 1946, 5, 20, 43.
9. Saarikangas 1993, 229–370; Saarikangas 2002, 350–379.
10. Ibid.
11. Ibid.; Helamaa 1983, 67–118.
12. Ibid.
13. Mandelin 1957, 57.
14. Aaltonen et al. (1960) 1961, 2–3, 21. From 1959 *Omakotikirja* was also sold as ten separate booklets.
15. Ahmavaara 1966.
16. Ahmavaara 1969; Anna-Liisa Ahmavaara was editor-in-chief of magazine *Kaunis Koti,* and her books were based on the presentations of the houses featured in it.
17. Sanaksenaho 2005, 22–26.
18. Lehtovuori 1984, 3.
19. Tallqvist 1986, 8, 22. English translation modified.
20. Lauronen 1991, 123–131; Rajanti 2004, 90–93.
21. Korpelainen 2005, 26.
22. Ibid., 20–22.

REFERENCES

Aaltonen, Irma; Ruusuvuori, Aarno; Tukkila, Iiro; Visanti, Markus (eds.): *Omakotikirja,* 3rd edition, Tammi, Helsinki 1961.

Ahmavaara, Anna-Liisa: *Living Close to Nature. Finnish Private Houses and Saunas*, Otava, Helsinki 1966.

Ahmavaara, Anna-Liisa: *Asumme omassa talossa,* Otava, Helsinki 1969.

Hautajärvi, Harri: "Plastic Bubbles and Capsule Homes. Architectural Utopias of the Space Age", *Futuro. Tomorrow's House from Yesterday*, eds. Marko Home, Mika Taanila, Desura, Helsinki 2002.

Helamaa, Erkki: *40-luku. Korsujen ja jälleenrakentamisen vuosikymmen*, Suomen rakennustaiteen museo, Helsinki 1983.

Huokuna, Tiina: *Vallankumous kotona! Arkielämän visuaalinen murros 1960-luvun lopussa ja 1970-luvun alussa*, Yliopistopaino, Helsinki 2006.

Huurre, Matti: *Kivikauden Suomi*, Otava, Helsinki 1998.

Korhonen, Teppo: "Kansanomainen rakennustaide keskiajalta 1800-luvun lopulle", *Ars. Suomen taide 3*, Weilin & Göös, Helsinki 1988.

Korpelainen, Heini: "Popular Culture of Detached Houses. Prefabricated Houses in the Whirlwind of Modern Industry and Tradition", *Arkkitehti – The Finnish Architectural Review*, 4/2005.

Lampi, Pertti: *Oma tupa – oma lupa. Omakotiliikkeen ja -rakentamisen sekä pientaloasumisen historiaa ja kehitysvaiheita*, Suomen Omakotiliitto ry, Helsinki 2007.

Latvala, Seppo: Internet articles on the Savo chimneyless cabin: <www.pohjois-savonmuisti.fi>, 2004.

Lauronen, Erja: *Unelma ja sen toteuttajat – tutkimus suomalaisista omakotirakentajista*, Asuntohallitus, tutkimus- ja suunnitteluosasto, Helsinki 1991.

Lehtovuori, Olli: *Hyvin suunniteltu pientalo*, Rakentajain Kustannus Oy, Helsinki 1984.

Mandelin, Walter: *Jokamiehen rakennusopas omakoti- ja talkoorakentajille*, WSOY, Porvoo–Helsinki, 1946.

Mandelin, Walter (ed.): *Jokamies rakentajana. Huvila- ja omakotirakentajan opas*, WSOY, Porvoo 1957.

Muurimäki, Eero: Internet articles on the Saarijärvi Stone Age village: <www.avoinmuseo.fi/kivikaudenkyla>, 2004.

Nurmi, Esko: *Alussa oli hellahuone. Asuntoreformiyhdistys 100 vuotta 1910–2010*, Asuntoreformiyhdistys ry, Helsinki 2010.

Rajanti, Taina: "Mitä omaa löytyy omakotitalosta?", *Oma koti. Omakotiasuminen Suomessa*, ed. Anna-Maija Halme, Suomen Kotiseutuliiton julkaisuja A:10, 2004.

Saarikangas, Kirsi: *Asunnon muodonmuutoksia. Puhtauden estetiikka ja sukupuoli modernissa arkkitehtuurissa*, Suomalaisen Kirjallisuuden Seura, Helsinki 2002.

Saarikangas, Kirsi: *Model Houses for Model Families. Gender, Ideology and the Modern Dwelling. The Type-Planned Houses of the 1940s in Finland*, Suomen Historiallinen Seura, Helsinki 1993.

Saarikangas, Kirsi: "Omakotitalon synty", *Oma koti. Omakotiasuminen Suomessa*, ed. Anna-Maija Halme, Suomen Kotiseutuliiton julkaisuja A:10, 2004.

Sanaksenaho, Pirjo: "Architects on Home Ground. Houses in the Finnish Architectural Review", *Arkkitehti – The Finnish Architectural Review*, 3/2003.

Tallqvist, Tore: "Small House Architecture and Tradition", *Finnish House*, Museum of Finnish Architecture, Helsinki 1986.

> Hvitträsk and Alvar Aalto's own house operate today as museums. Also Villa Mairea is open to the public. The Niemelä croft and Pertinotša house can be visited at the Seurasaari Open Air Museum in Helsinki. Villa Solin is owned by the City of Turku and used for civic receptions.

STUDIO WIDNÄS
FISKARS

The timber house and studio belonging to the artist Karin Widnäs was built on Hasselbacka hill at the outer edge of the historical Fiskars ironworks in 2005. The house also functions as the artist's experimental laboratory for ceramic products such as bricks, profiled and flat tiles, tiles for stoves, as well as handbasins.

The basic shape of the house, comprising three parts – a studio, home and sauna, with a floor area of 350 m^2 – shows how the surrounding nature has been utilised. A copper-clad mono-pitched roof acts as a unifying element, while the two-storey timber-clad enclosed elements help organise the space, and shelter the north side of both the studio and main living space of the home, with the windows on the ground floor on that side being as small as possible.

The third part of the original composition has later been built next to the house, a turf-roofed log sauna. In the traditional way, the water is carried into the sauna in buckets. The water from washing is absorbed into the ground through gaps between the floor planks, which at the same time guarantee efficient ventilation in the sauna.

TUOMO SIITONEN, ARCHITECT

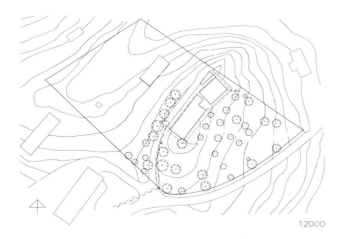

1:2000

The large, copper-clad monopitch roof dominates the exterior appearance of the building. Wild plants grow in the surrounding garden and the artist's two sheep keep the grass short.

The roofed outdoor space between the studio and the living quarters acts as a both a terrace and open-air gallery, with natural light entering the space indirectly from the windows above.

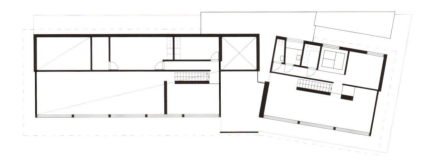

1ST FLOOR 1:300

GROUND FLOOR 1:300

43

The ceramic building parts and artworks by Karin Widnäs enhance the interior mood. The white easy chairs and foot stools, together with the small chairs by Kari Virtanen and Mikko Merz and the lamp by Camilla Moberg complement the spacious and light architecture of the interior.

Energy for heating the house is produced by geo-thermal energy and heat-storing ovens clad with ceramic tiles made by Widnäs. All other bricks and ceramic tiles used for various surfaces have also been made in Widnäs's workshop.

A draught lobby connects the living section to the outdoor gallery. The ceramic tiles on the end wall of the living room create variation in the otherwise simple space.

The first floor study is an open gallery that links to the studio space.

The external wall of the 2-storey section of the house was built from sturdy spruce planks. The different types of wood were selected to withstand the climate without the need for surface treatments and to achieve a grey patina over time. Ecological wood-fibre insulation has been used throughout. Also the roofs were built from natural materials such as copper and tarred aspen shingles.

VILLA LENA
ESPOO

The house is a study of a single space in the form of a residential unit. The concept for the design was that the exterior and interior spaces would form a single entity, while the gardens would act as intermediary zones between the building and the surrounding nature. The walls facing the gardens are transparent while those facing the neighbours and the street are solid. Inside the house, individual spaces are not exactly marked out and there are no acoustic barriers. Thin curtains and independent building parts mark the boundaries of the residents' private areas. The floor area of the house is 220 m².

The idea behind choosing certain rough material was to create connections with nature: the interior of the house is lined with fine-sawn T&G boarding and the floor is mechanically polished concrete with both clear and blue glass added to the mix. The frame of the building was constructed from prefabricated units, whereas the interior lining and exterior cladding were installed on site. Siberian larch was used for the exterior cladding.

Villa Lena, completed in 2003, was my own home until I moved into the next house I designed, Kotilo House.

OLAVI KOPONEN, ARCHITECT

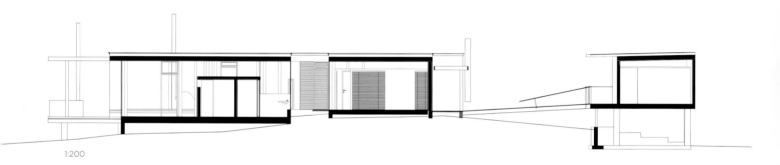

1:200

The house has been beautifully adapted to its surroundings that have been left in a natural state. The separate studio stands on concrete stilts and faces towards the evening sun beyond the main building. Below the studio are car-parking spaces.

1:1500

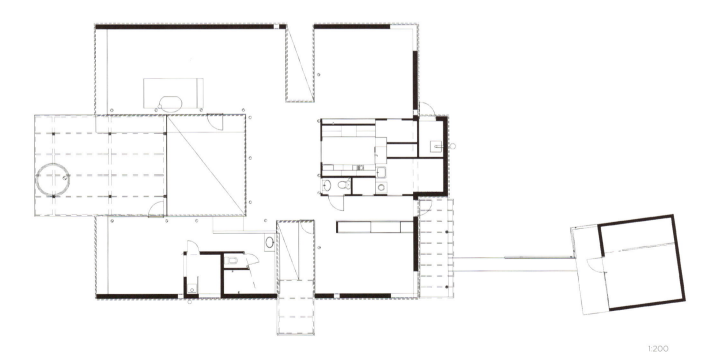

1:200

53

The aspen-shingle-clad sauna as seen from the bedroom. Beyond the sauna are two bathrooms. With the view from the bathroom into the south garden, morning ablutions are always a pleasure.

The fireplace was built by mason Tarmo Piri on the basis of a scale model. The table and chairs designed by Yrjö Kukkapuro in the 1960s were acquired second-hand.

KOTILO HOUSE
ESPOO

The idea of the house is a spiralling space [kotilo means 'gastropod' or 'conch'] derived from the overall form and materials. Thus of central importance are the experience of space, the path of light in the building, the various smells and the rhythm of the seasons and time of day. The objectives were freedom and effortlessness. In order for the architectural design to create the conditions for a multi-faceted life, I had given thought to what people actually do at home – alone or with others. I had been thinking about the themes of both celebrations and everyday life.

Feelings of homeliness, naturalness and an obviousness emerging from simplicity are the most important features of vernacular architecture. It combines modest materials, craftsmanship and a folk wisdom arising from life's experiences. It is the opposite of academic theory, a burden I inevitably carry as an architect. Kotilo House may well be an unconscious attempt to combine these aspects. It also differs in an important way from my earlier work: the connection to nature is present mainly at the level of associations.

In terms of building construction, the house has been very demanding in regard to both the structural frame and the surfaces. The basic structure consists of 180 wooden floor, wall and roof elements that spiral around a central concrete flue and which are partially supported by steel structures. The exterior shingles are larch and the interior shingles are aspen. The foundations and ground floor surfaces are concrete.

Kotilo House is completely handmade. The 210 m² house did not exceed the average price per square metre for a detached house. Affordability was achieved through the particular choice of structural solutions. Kotilo House, completed in 2006, was built as my own home in the low-rise residential area of Kauklahti in Espoo.

OLAVI KOPONEN, ARCHITECT

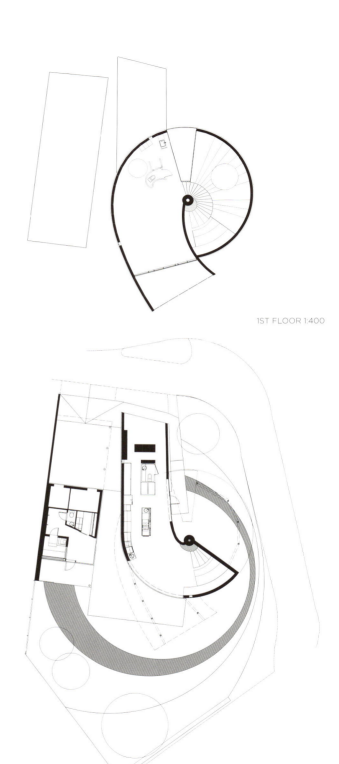

1ST FLOOR 1:400

GROUND FLOOR 1:400

61

The floor levels are terraced like a vineyard. In the curved section of the ceiling every shingle is individually cut to the correct shape.

The main entrance is located below a recess. The glass external wall on the ground floor features a glass mosaic by artist Lauri Ahlgrén.

The spiral house is located at the curved end of the neighbourhood block. There is a view southwards from the upper floor. The utility outbuilding that marks the plot border is separated from the main house by a gap of only around one metre.

The large upper floor balcony and glass wall are oriented southwards, with a view of the landscape between the neighbouring buildings.

The upstairs bathroom is open to the adjacent room. The WC and shower are situated in an internal "hut".

TAMMIMÄKI HOUSE
LIPPAJÄRVI, ESPOO

The Lippajärvi region in Espoo belongs to a rare type of habitat in Finland, a broad-leaved deciduous woodland characterized by oaks and maples. The plot of the house slopes down towards the west, and the nearby lake can be glimpsed between the trees. The house is situated perpendicular to the slope, so that when viewed from the top of the slope the longish building mass appears to be a single-storey building, while when viewed from the base of the slope one sees the two residential floors plus a further basement storage level.

The overall form of the house has been inspired by a one-hundred year old oak tree that grows on the site. The long south facade on the garden side has been bent into a curve, such that the curved wooden decking and terraced lawn surround the old tree like annual growth rings. The terrace and first floor balcony catch the sunlight throughout the day, from the early morning to the late evening.

The house is home for our five-member family. Its scale ranges from the small and intimate to the tall and festive. The total floor area is 150 m². In the main space we strived to attain the spirit of a traditional farmhouse with its combined kitchen and living room. Through the choice of both form and materials we wanted to create a humane and comfortable home environment.

MATTI AND PIRJO SANAKSENAHO, ARCHITECTS

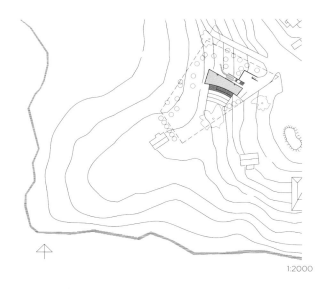

1:2000

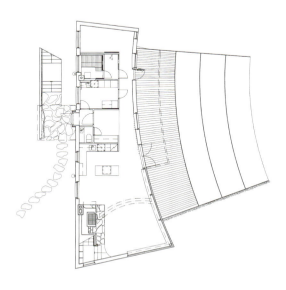

GROUND FLOOR 1:300

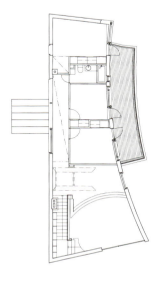

1ST FLOOR 1:300

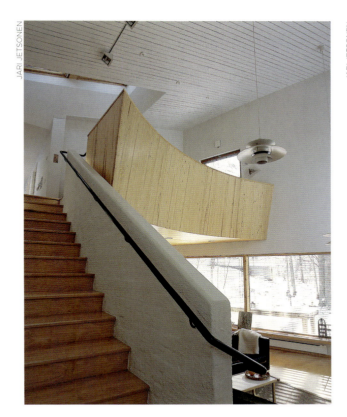

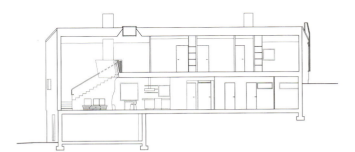

1:300

The family prepare food, eat and spend time together in the same large space. The fireplace is the focal point of the interior, and the living room as well as details such as the stairs and bookshelf built into it are organised around it.

The living room is double height. The gallery overlooking the room is used as a work space. Its curved timber balustrade – built from glulam pine with a waxed finish – forms an internal facade or "bow end of a boat". The ceiling is clad with sawn timber boarding. A roof light provides natural light in the space.

The house is located on a slope facing south-west. The garden is terraced in front of a great oak tree. All the upper floor rooms have access to the common balcony. The curved facade, terrace and balcony form an "auditorium" overlooking the garden. The living room and dining space have double doors opening on to the terrace. A bench for cooling off after a sauna is placed against the wall below the balcony. The house, completed in 2001, has since then acquired a beautiful grey patina.

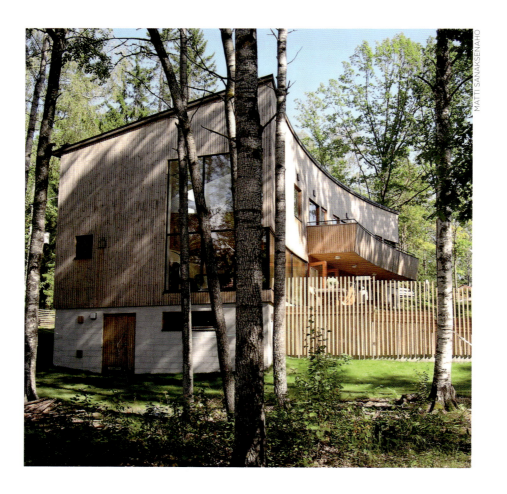

LAULUMAA HOUSE
OULAINEN

The house is situated on the bank of the Pyhäjoki River. On the south-west side, facing towards the river, is a large glazed facade, while the facades on the northern sides have only small windows. Accordingly, the house has a sheltered rear side and an open front side oriented towards the sun. The window facade is sheltered, however, from the peak summer sunshine by a colonnaded canopy – a Finnish version of the more southern loggias.

The house has a timber construction, with cellulose fibre thermal insulation. The facades are clad with planed wood weather-boarding cut to a specific shape. The internal walls are clad with plywood.

Heating is provided by an air-water heat pump and a heat-storing fireplace in the living room, the firewood for which is taken from the plot. In addition to the combined living room and kitchen and bedroom on the ground-floor, there is also a large two-part loft space.

Surrounding the house and all the way up to the bank of the river is a natural meadow. The rainwater from the roof is used to water the plants in the garden.

LAURI LOUEKARI, ARCHITECT

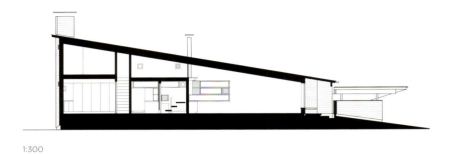

1:300

The construction of the house consists of a timber frame clad on the exterior with 150 x 28 mm horizontal weatherboarding as well as stained plywood. The house was completed in 2009, and has a floor area of 94 m².

In the centre of the living room is a heat-storing brick fireplace that is in frequent use. The wood for the fire comes from trees on the plot of the house.

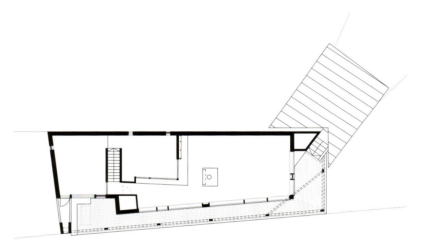

1ST FLOOR 1:300

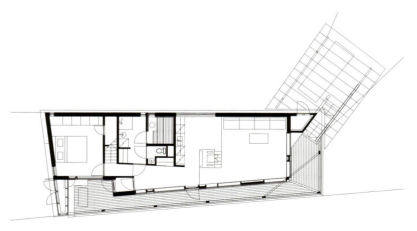

GROUND FLOOR 1:300

FONI HOUSE
OULU

The central theme in the design of the house was the use of natural light. The idea of an "instrument of light", in which the spaces oriented in different directions transform as the direction and intensity of light changes in accordance with the rhythm of the day, was based on the family's musical interests. The building has a shallow plan, and therefore light flows into the rooms from many directions.

The spatial character of the living room and music room changes from the general rectangular form of the rest of the house to a conically opening space; viewed from the main entrance, the space expands both horizontally and vertically. The architecture of the exterior has references to an animal figure; the gables open up as tall face-like glass surfaces, while the recesses and projections stand out from the white "skin" as separate organs.

The L-shaped plan of the house helps to shelter the courtyard from the cold north winds coming in from the nearby Toppilansaari seafront. On the north side of the house there are only narrow windows that follow the direction of the façade boarding, while there are larger windows on the sides of the house facing other directions. Particularly the windows overlooking the courtyard and the west-facing window wall function in the spring and autumn as passive solar heat collectors.

ANNA LOUEKARI AND LAURI LOUEKARI, ARCHITECTS

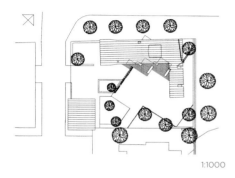

1:1000

In the interior, plywood and wooden panelling have partly been placed in front of the gypsum-faced walls for acoustic reasons and to increase the sense of comfort. Aspen wood, waxed or with a translucent finish, has been used for the bookshelves and other fixed furniture in the living room. There is a view of the sea through the tall window, both from the ground floor and from the upstairs bedroom via the living room.

The house, completed in 2004, was specifically designed for a cold and windy climate. The sheltered south yard is well suited as a place to sit outside. The house, with a floor area of 266 m², has a timber construction and cellulose fibre insulation.

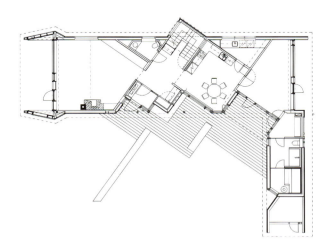

GROUND FLOOR 1:300

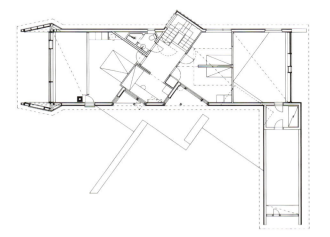

1ST FLOOR 1:300

VILLA LEPOLA
ESPOO

The site is relatively small and sloping, but with the house located as close as possible to the northeast and southeast boundaries a verdant open garden is formed on the lake side to the west. The rooms open out on to the garden and also enjoy views of the lake between the trees.

The approach to the house is from the highest point of the site, in the eastern corner. A plan with an unusual number of changes of level for a single-storey house has been created, where the spaces interlock with each other, flowing down, almost unimpeded, from one level to another to the basement. The floor area of the house is 197 m².

The row of bedrooms and the small-windowed kitchen along the street side protect the meandering living room areas, offering an unlimited number of different views inside the house, lengthwise and diagonally, from one space to another, as well as down, up and out to the landscape. The interiors have literally become a part of the landscape.

JUHA LEIVISKÄ, ARCHITECT AND TAPANI SCHRODERUS, ARCHITECTURE STUDENT

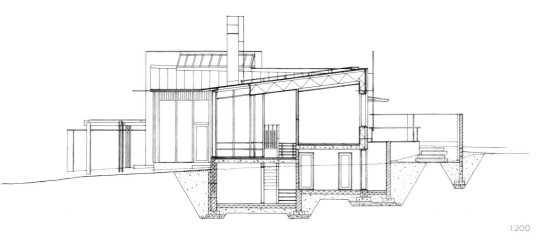

1:200

The large windows give a feeling of a direct connection between the living room and dining space and the nature in the garden.
A slender stairs links together the interior spaces.

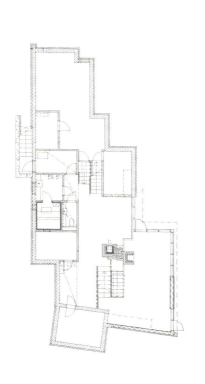

BASEMENT 1:300

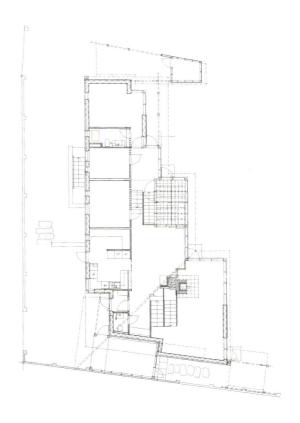

GROUND FLOOR 1:300

On the garden side of the house there is a view from the large windows across the lake-side road towards the lake. The street-side façade, protected by a wall, feels more enclosed.

The house, completed in 1999, has become part of the landscape.

SJÖBODA HOUSE
SIPOO

The south sloping rocky shoreline plot, dominated by pine trees and rich in vegetation yet nevertheless fragile, set strict limits on the design of the house. The houses in the area are modest in scale. They are positioned in a random chain-like formation further away from the shoreline, on the upper parts of narrow plots of land, while their small sheds and saunas are situated closer to the water. The wooden buildings subtly follow the topography and they have a harmonious relationship with the nature.

We followed these environmental building principles when designing the new house. By folding the new building into three units, each of which correspond to the size of the existing houses in the area, it was possible to smoothly adapt the building to the height variations of the site without cuts in the terrain or terracing.

Together with the new building, two rocky outcrops at the north end of the site delineate the entrance courtyard in the manner of a traditional Finnish farmhouse yard. The middle and lower parts of the site, characterised by exposed smooth-faced bedrock, were left in their natural state.

When selecting the location of the house from the premise of preserving nature, the potential offered by the site could be exploited also in the interior. This is apparent in the spatial connections and vistas both inside the building and out into nature and the landscape.

JUHA LEIVISKÄ AND ROSEMARIE SCHNITZLER, ARCHITECTS

1:2000

An extensive view opens up from the living room towards the shoreline. Light enters the space also from upper windows on the opposite side of the room. The interior spaces flow into one another, are subdivided on several levels and link directly to the terrain and landscape on both sides of the building. The house, completed in 2004, has a floor area of 240 m².

The house feels less open on the entrance court side than on the shoreline side with its large windows the full height of the room. The brick selected for the house is a reflection of the red and grey tones of the dominant rock in the area.

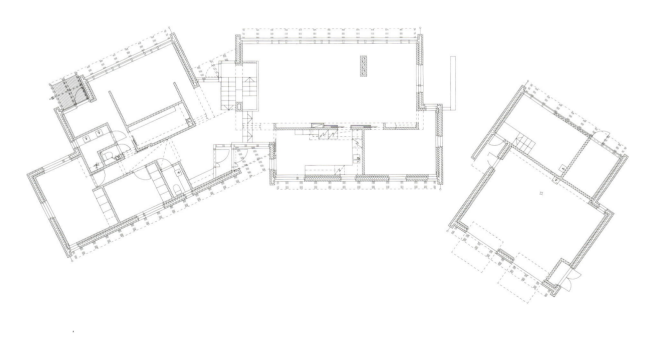

GROUND FLOOR 1:250

MOBY DICK
ESPOO

The house with a biomorphic form peers out from behind a rock along the street. One enters the house through the white free-form wall, a stone stairway and steel bridge leading to the main entrance on the first floor. Also on the same floor as the entrance are the living room and kitchen as well as a library, the parents' bedroom and two external balconies. On the ground floor are the children's rooms, a guest room and the garage. In the basement are the sauna, a sauna lounge and gym. The house has a total floor area of 262 m².

A tall stairwell links together the floors as well as a two-storey-high winter garden. These are pierced by translucent glass and steel bridges. A large skylight brings light into the central stairwell that functions as the spatial core of the house. From the stairs one can see into all the most important rooms either directly or via glazed walls, each with different types of glass. The staircase acts as a free-form steel sculpture, its slenderness attempting to defy gravity.

The double curved ceiling on the first-floor complements the spatial totality created by the free forms. All the partition walls are straight, providing a dynamic series of lines within the subdivision of the house.

JYRKI TASA AND TUOMAS UUSHEIMO, ARCHITECTS

PHOTOS JUSSI TIAINEN

1ST FLOOR 1:500

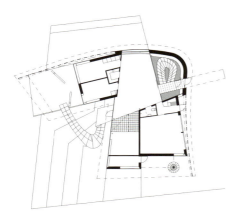

GROUND FLOOR 1:500

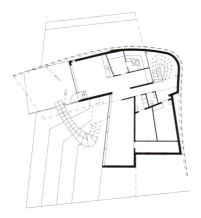

BASEMENT 1:500

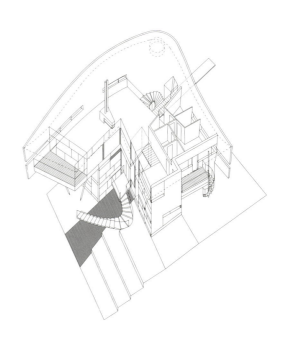

The free-form steel tentacles of the stairs appear to defy gravity. The upper surface of the hollow steel stair structure has been lined with solid oak. The railing is made of steel cable.

The large living room space is divided by the aluminium-faced, steel-framed fireplace. The two-storey conservatory, which separates the kitchen from the living room, can be seen in the background. The ceiling is built with lap-jointed birch plywood boarding, enabling the double curve.

The free form, oblique white plywood-clad wall dominates the exterior, and the same wall is white also in the interior. The other facades are clad in plywood and pine battens. The exuberant, unconventional house was completed in 2003, but in its uniqueness is timeless.

The white curved facade on the entrance side conceals the vivid massing on the garden side. The first floor deck extends towards the evening sun and shelters the cooling-off terrace of the sauna below.
The structure of the building consists of steel columns, composite steel and concrete floor slabs with a steel and timber roof structure. The gently rising stone stair and steel bridge lead to the main entrance on the first floor.

INTO HOUSE
ESPOO

The house is located on a high hill facing west, towards the sea. The approach road leads to the white protective facade. The undulating eaves and tall, oblique steel columns of the opposite, west side are only partially visible, giving a hint of the dual character of the house. The visitor crosses a steel bridge above a pool and arrives at a tall glass cut in the white wall, which marks the location of the main entrance.

On entering the building there opens immediately a view through the tall glazed external wall to the large terrace and the sea. The high-ceilinged entrance hall forms the heart of the house. The entire house can be perceived and grasped from the entrance hall. The bedrooms, the sauna and the swimming pool are situated on the entrance floor. On the upper floor are the kitchen with the adjacent dining area and balcony which receives the morning sun, and the living room with its balcony towards the afternoon sun.

The structure of the house consists of a steel framework with connecting wooden frames and beams. The basement and the tower are built in reinforced concrete. Horizontal bracing is provided by the tower and the curving external wall.

The house was designed for a bachelor, but also provides an excellent setting for socialising. The living areas are spacious, while the bedrooms and utility areas are relatively small.

JYRKI TASA, ARCHITECT

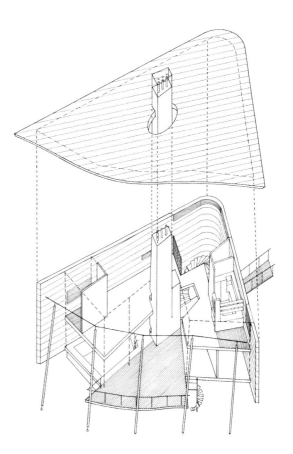

PHOTOS JUSSI TIAINEN

The structure of the house consists of a main steel frame with connecting wooden frame and beam systems. The vertical steel structures are oblong or round-profile tubing, while the horizontal ones are open-profile beams. The system of wooden roof beams is supported by round stainless steel columns and steel beams. The rear facade is clad with white-painted vertical weatherboarding, and the seafront facade with high-profile battening and pine plywood.

The curved white wall appears to shelter the warm, wood-clad dwelling, while turning its back towards the cold north.

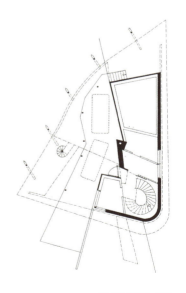 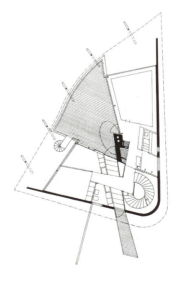 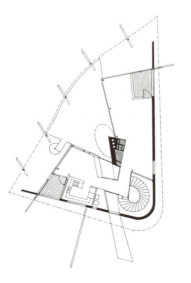

BASEMENT 1:400   GROUND FLOOR 1:400   FIRST FLOOR 1:400

The materials and details closest to the dweller are an essential element in architecture. A central aim was to find a balance between large, clear elements and small details. The latter include door handles and railings and, for instance, the mechanism of the glazed sliding doors leading to the balcony. The handling of the materials – wood, metal, and glass – was kept as simple as possible.

The house was completed in 1998, but the polymorphic architecture is timeless. The emphasis in the design of the 173 m² house has been put on the spacious living areas

The sculptural steel and wood staircase winds up through three storeys. The folded plywood steps with varying radius are supported by lightweight steel tubing and cable structures. Light filters into the staircase through a three-storey glass-brick wall.

ERIKSSON HOUSE
VAASA

The single-family house stands beside the sea in the middle of an area of summer cottages of all ages and styles. A functionalist-style summer cottage on the site, badly beyond repair, was demolished to make way for the new house. The two-storey cube-like part of the building is a re-incarnated 'cottage' that supports a single-storey wall-like wing.

The rooms look out towards a beautiful seascape. The surrounding landscape and natural light flood in from all four sides of the white cube, comprising a work space on the upper floor – which in turn overlooks the living room below – colouring the interior space with changing tones and moods.

The building has a timber frame, partly faced with brick, which has then been rendered, and partly clad with timber boarding. The landscape windows on the ground floor were set directly into the prefabricated frame in order to create a feeling of delicate spaciousness.

HEIKKI AITOAHO AND KAARLO VILJANEN, ARCHITECTS

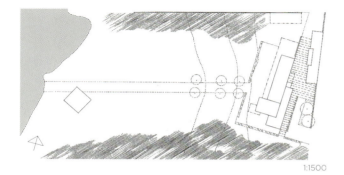

1:1500

PHOTOS JUSSI TIAINEN

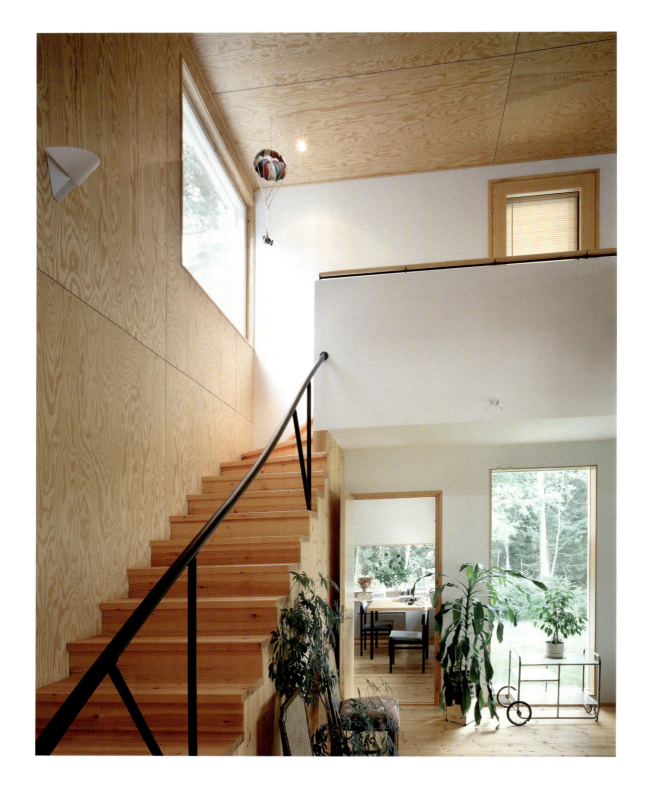

GROUND FLOOR 1:400

The upper floor of the white cube contains a space that overlooks the living room below.

The plan of the house, completed in 1998, is distinct: the total 134 m² is divided into a white two-storey cube-like volume and a low wing. The former contains the living and work spaces and the latter the kitchen and bedrooms. The stairs leads to the gallery floor. Both the ceiling and the walls are untreated conifer plywood.

VILLA SMEDJEBACKA
LAIHIA

The house is situated in a rarer variation of the traditional Ostrobothnian landscape, one surrounded by large spruce trees and boulders. The buildings belonging to an old small-holding on the plot had already collapsed before the design work began. The neighbouring houses represent almost all types of post-war residential building up to the present day. Therefore the ideology and references for the design of the house did not have to be the adaptation to the surroundings. Instead we chose to create a modern connection to the forest.

Each tree and boulder that showed some sign of vibrancy was preserved. In front of the building is a paved yard demarcated by outbuildings. The entrance to the yard is guarded by an enormous lighting-struck spruce tree which brings colour and atmosphere to most of the rooms in the house. The floor area in the spacious house is 218 m^2. The main living spaces mainly oriented towards the setting sun and the sheltered rear yard. Their peaceful atmosphere is due to the natural light entering from several directions and also the classical Finnish interior design.

In terms of the overall architecture, the objective has been a timeless Finnish-Scandinavian modernism, a central aim of which to grasp and capture natural light in the interior throughout the year.

HEIKKI AITOAHO AND KAARLO VILJANEN, ARCHITECTS

PHOTOS JUSSI TIAINEN

The dining space, living room and library form an uninterrupted space offering varying moods and angles into the yard. The windows, doors and the many pieces of fixed furniture are local workmanship.

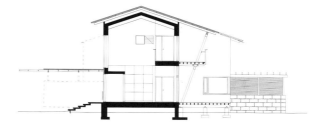

1:300

GROUND FLOOR 1:300

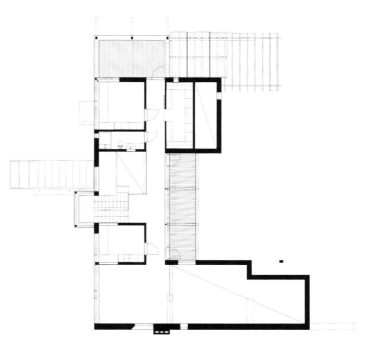

1ST FLOOR 1:300

The building is oriented towards the afternoon and evening sun. Even during the summer there is no manicured lawn to maintain. The boulders and stone walls have mostly been shaped on site. The classically modernistic house, completed in 2006, has preserved its timeless stamp.

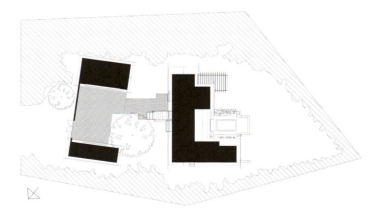

1:1000

MELIN HOUSE
VAASA

The house is located at the edge of an area of single-family houses built in various styles and surrounded by forest. The L-shaped building and separate garage together with the forest edge delimit a sheltered yard area, into which all the main living spaces overlook.

Despite its contemporary spirit, the house attempts, with its pitched roof and colours, to socialize with its neighbours. The total floor area of the house is 148 m². The overall spatial concept is defined by a series of spaces, formed by the rooms, with the light and materials creating a particular mood depending on the season and time of day. Most of the rooms have views out in at least two directions, as well as into other rooms. The interior walls surfaces are lacquered conifer and oil-painted gypsum boarding.

The starting point in the design was to create a healthy house, with breathable constructions, such as the traditional crawl-space under the floor, and without using plastics or mineral wool. Tried-and-tested materials were chosen, such as wood and brick, and finishing materials with a pleasant aroma for both the interior and exterior.

**HEIKKI AITOAHO AND
KAARLO VILJANEN, ARCHITECTS**

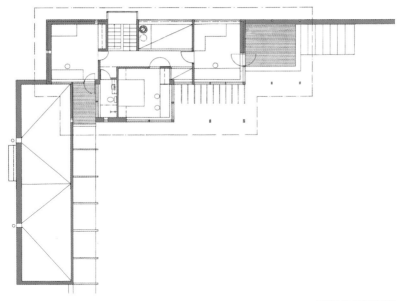

The house, completed in 1997, is set naturally in its surroundings. The calm, down-to-earth colouring and traditional pitched roof give a feeling of harmony. The facades are brick with either a bagged or rendered finish and wood treated with wood oil and tar.

In addition to the main garden, there is an abundance of different exterior spaces around the house. Marking the edge of the garden is a conservatory, which is a continuation of the library. Above the library, in turn, is a balcony adjoining a bedroom. The main entrance is sheltered by a glass roof supported by beams.

FIRST FLOOR 1:300

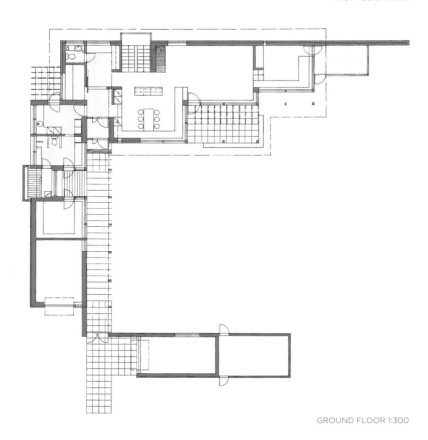

GROUND FLOOR 1:300

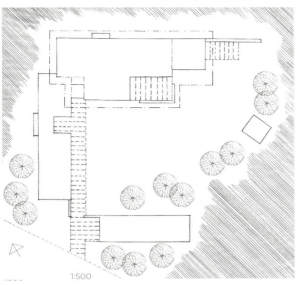

KEKKAPÄÄ HOUSE
ESPOO

We built a house for our family in a cultural-historically significant agricultural landscape in north Espoo. The existing buildings in the area were a significant inspiration for the character of the house and choice of building materials. The simple form, topped with a pitched roof, integrates the house into its environment.

The west-facing slope of the woodland site is divided into two areas of differing character; the lower part comprised of a heath-like forest and the upper part with pine forest and moss-covered rocky ground. The front yard comprises the main entrance, children's play area, outside terrace and a workshop. On the opposite side of the main building, with a more fragile nature, is a solitary path leading to the sauna building.

The sloping site where the two-storey house is positioned was partly excavated so that there is access from both floors into the surroundings. The 282 m² main building comprises three zones: living and working spaces and a glass-roofed conservatory linking the two, which also acts as the meeting room for our office. The office space faces north and east and could later be transformed into a separate apartment. An open kitchen, living room and balcony oriented towards the evening sun are situated on the upper floor. The ground floor is reserved for the bedrooms, a gym and children's play space.

KATARIINA RAUTIALA AND PENTTI RAISKI, ARCHITECTS

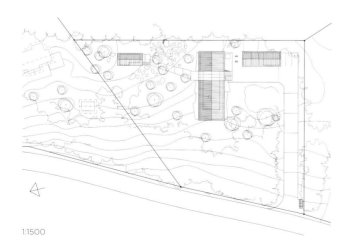

1:1500

The balcony and access gallery extend the living space out into the surrounding countryside. Yrjö Kukkapuro's Carousel chairs were rescued from a landfill site and repaired.

On the lower floor, which is partly sunken into the rock, are the bedrooms, children's play area and gym.

BASEMENT 1:400

GROUND FLOOR 1:400

The table in the space between the dwelling and workspace is made from a birch tree that grew on the site. The walls are lined with spruce boarding given a translucent finish.

The house has a unified timber frame system with wood wool insulation. Free-standing glulam columns and tension bars at the ends of the building give the frame the required stiffness.

On the upper floor are the open kitchen, living room and balcony oriented towards the evening sun. The structural glulam members, made to order from thin pine lamellae, have been left exposed.

The house, completed in 2006, is designed also with the future in mind. The northeast-oriented office space can be transformed into a separate dwelling. The waxed and polished wooden window frames are fitted to the jambs with birch plywood surrounds.

A timber plank walkway-terrace leads to the sauna. The walkway protects the ground from wear and tear and hides the service connections to the sauna. Nature was carefully protected during construction. The facades of the 23 m² sauna are clad with weatherboarding treated with a mix of wood tar and preservative.

PÄIVÄRINNE HOUSE
SALO

The house I designed for my family is situated at the southern edge of the city of Salo. The house is built on the site of the old Päivärinne apple farm, on the summit of a south-facing slope, and is surrounded by traditional war-veteran houses and typical rural houses. Consequently, the design turned out as a simple, pitched-roofed wooden house. It was completed in 2008 and has a floor area of 200 m^2. Due to the shallow building frame, all the rooms face south, towards the valley landscape. The bedrooms were designed to be flexible. The size and number of rooms can be altered fairly easily.

The house fulfils the requirements of a low-energy building. This was achieved by extra insulation, an efficient ventilation system with a heat recovery unit, and by orienting the windows (with a good U-Value) optimally for light and heat. In the construction particular attention was paid to the air-tightness of the building envelope. The main building material is wood, with wood-based insulation.

The house has two heat-storing fireplaces as well as direct electric under-floor heating. A virtue of the under-floor heating is that the indoor temperature can be slightly lower without compromising on comfort. In the design I also made provision for the future utilisation of solar energy.

The location was of great significance when searching for a site. Though the house is situated in the suburbs the Salo city centre is only 4,5 kilometres away. The journey is easily completed by bicycle.

SANTERI LIPASTI, ARCHITECT

1ST FLOOR 1:250

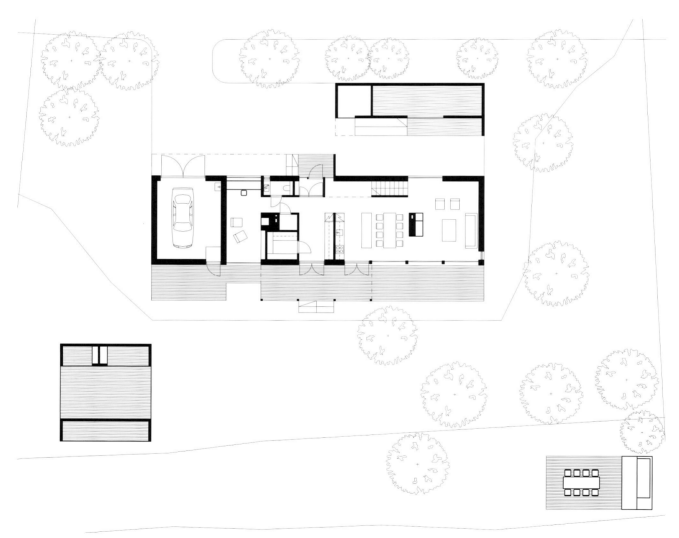

GROUND FLOOR 1:250

The wooden facades are given a so-called "Roslag mahogany" treatment, a finish made from a mixture of linseed oil and tar.

1:400

The living spaces are open plan. A starting point in the design was the view towards the garden and valley in the south. The room height is low – only 2.5 metres – and the purpose is to direct attention out into the landscape. At the same time, the rooms become intimate and pleasant.

The fireplaces incorporate a secondary air-intake designed by fireplace researcher and designer Heikki Hyytiäinen, which gives clean burning and small particle emissions.

The covered terrace can be used up until late autumn.

The children's rooms on the first floor are pleasant spaces full of natural light. The mirror on the rear wall and the large windows create the illusion of a space continuing to infinity.

The house's second heat-storing fireplace is in the comfortable living room. The rear wall is clad in knot-free pine panelling.

VILLA AAMUTUULI
ESPOO

I designed Villa Aamutuuli for my own family over a period of two years, although it took only three months to build. The 88,5 m² house is designed for two adults and one child, but there is room for beds for seven persons, if necessary. My starting points were beauty and lightness, the combination of wood and glass as well as the continuity and spaciousness of the rooms. The objectives guiding the design process were also efficiency and cost management.

Villa Aamutuuli is located in Friisilä, an area of war-veteran houses in Espoo from the 1940s and 1950s. The house is placed so as to maximise the area of the back garden, out into which the rooms open, and to make it as sheltered as possible.

The house is a variation of the open platform timber frame system, and all the timber parts were delivered from the supplier pre-planned, at a specified time, cut to size and packed.

The interior is characterised by warm and clearly delineated wood surfaces. Untreated, fine-sawn, exterior-quality boarding was used for the ceiling, and the rooms have mainly birch parquet flooring.

ASKO KINNUNEN, ARCHITECT

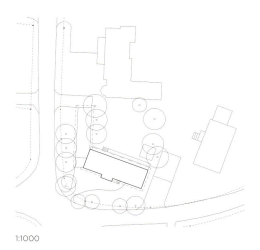

1:1000

PHOTOS JARI JETSONEN

1:200   1:200

All main spaces of the house overlook the garden and the entire façade on that side is glazed. The other three facades are clad with horizontal 170 x 28 mm weatherboarding. The house turns its back to the street, and the windows are small or placed high beneath the roof line.

The house, completed in 2005, is by modern standards a small house. There is still space for a 80 m² extension, if needed.

The parents' bedroom opens out through French doors on to a sheltered terrace. The dining group makes an attractive breakfast spot in the summer.

The upper strip window on the street side of the house lets in light at ceiling height. The workroom, parents' bedroom, kitchen and living room are, in practice, a single open space that continues through the house to the children's bedroom. The spaces are separated only by frosted glass sliding doors.

VILLA INKERI
HEINOLA

The house, designed for a family that spends their leisure time being active, is a combination of contemporary architecture and traditional building. On the upper slope of the plot is a car part, from where there is a connection by bridge to the main building. The modern main building and the log guest cabin and sauna together form a sheltered yard that opens out towards a forested lake landscape.

The heat-storing massive concrete frame of the lower floor was cast on site. The visible surfaces were treated with opaque silicate paint to highlight the wood grain pattern of the shuttering boards. The doors and windows were hand-made by a joiner, and the orange-toned varnish stands out against the wooden facades that will turn grey with time.

The logs for the guest cabin and sauna were Karelian so-called Kelo-wood from standing dead pine trees, hand-hewn on two sides by axe, and with short dovetail jointed corners. The implementation tested how well the traditional log-jointing techniques are suited for the expression of modern architecture. The internal walls and ceilings as well as all fixed furniture were hand-made by a carpenter from birch plywood, given a thin white waxed finish. The house is heated using geothermal heating, heat storing stoves and, if needed, electricity.

HANNU KIISKILÄ, ARCHITECT

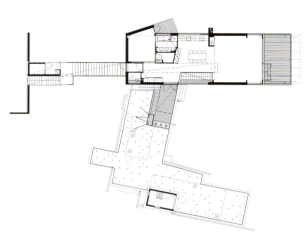

FIRST FLOOR 1:400

BASEMENT 1:400

A view framed by the wooden battened walls of the terrace opens up from the spacious living space towards Suurijärvi Lake. The house, completed in 2009, has a floor area of 274 m².

During warm evenings, the lower floor kitchen-lounge, separated from the terrace by sliding glass doors, becomes virtually an outdoor living-dining space for the family.

The facades, bridges and terraces were built from yellow cedar, a species used for North American Native Indian totem poles, which contains natural pesticides preventing the growth of tree rot.

VILLA SARI
PORI

The building is located in the Ruosniemi housing area in Pori. The site is on a rocky ridge running in an east-west direction towards the sea, where there has been human settlement since the Bronze Age.

The most important wishes of the client family were to extend the living spaces outdoors, the creation of a natural link between the house and the surrounding rounded rock outcrops, as well as the provision of an abundance of views.

The centrally-placed open kitchen divides the house and the yard spaces into separate sections, each with its own character. The children's rooms located on the north side were raised slightly above the other spaces, thus giving them good views to the upper yard and fields via inner windows. The sauna section includes a veranda where bathers can cool off. A gallery space linked to the living room on the upper storey provides extra ventilation in summer and can be used as guest accommodation.

An improvement of about 20% in the energy balance was achieved by means of additional insulation, selective low-energy glazing and heat-recovery equipment. The timber construction was complemented with glulam and laminated veneer lumber structures.

HANNU KIISKILÄ, ARCHITECT

Villa Sari was especially designed to exploit the low angle of the winter sun in Finland. In summer, shade is created with canopies and adjustable wooden louvers made of yellow cedar. The house, completed in 1997, has a floor area of 279 m², which enabled a generously dimensioned living room and dining area, placed with their adjacent terraces facing the evening sun.

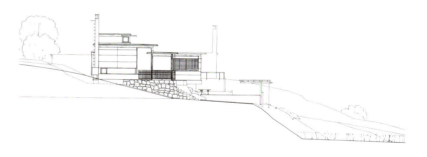

1:400

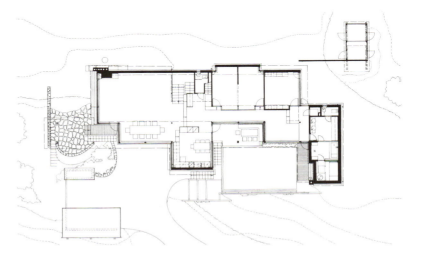

1:400

PHOTOS JUHANI KARANKA

VERSTA HOUSE
HYVINKÄÄ

The house was built in 2008 on an old garden plot in a suburb of Hyvinkää, as the home of an elderly couple. The building continues the tradition of modern house design established by Alvar Aalto.

The clients' wish for a 'tiny' and simple home was materialised as an airy 143 m² dwelling in a humane scale and with beautiful and functional rooms. The course of the day and change in light on the site as well as the swing motion in golf, which is the clients' hobby, inspired the shape of the building and its spatial layout.

The heart of the house is the sun terrace in the courtyard, which is sheltered from the gaze of passers by along the street. Here it is possible to spend the warmest part of the day and admire the apple orchard.

TITTA TAMMINEN AND JUHANI KARANKA, ARCHITECTS

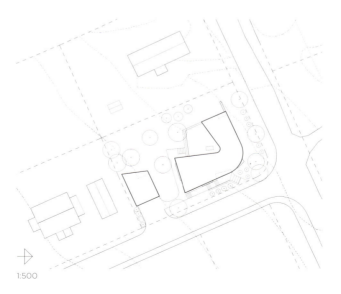

1:500

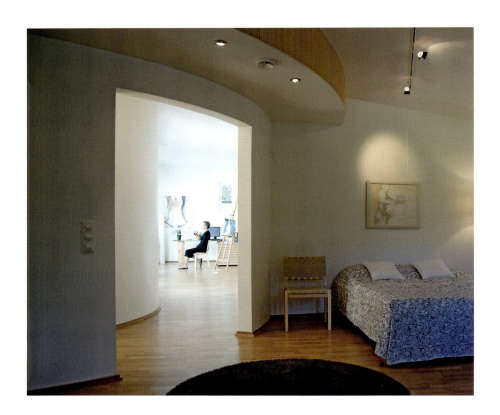

The intimate, dusky cave-like bedroom is not isolated from the free-flowing overlapping spaces of the house.

The living room is the largest and tallest space in the house, containing a fireplace, a connection out to the terrace, as well as a French balcony facing south. The principal colours used in the building, white and oak, are also dominant here.

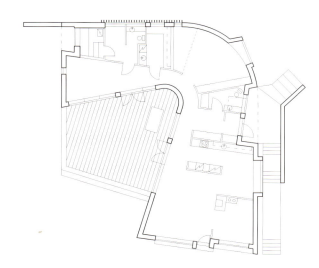

1:300

The main spaces and terrace are oriented towards the warming southern sunlight. During the spring and summer, the old, twisted apple trees cast playful shadows on the plastered walls of the house, shielding it from the worst heat of the sun. It was decided not to place a canopy on the terrace.

The bay window jutting out from the outer curved wall captures the first light of dawn. The old maple trees, lilacs and Burnet roses continue to grow along the boundary between this former garden plot and the road to the north.

ALANEN HOUSE
KIRKKONUMMI

The house, completed in 2004, is located on a beautiful, southward sloping site. The upper part of the plot is moss-covered rock while the lower part is lusher, with spruce trees and an undergrowth of blueberry bushes.

The client couple wanted to live in a spacious house characterised by light colours, with a narrow-framed, L-shaped plan. All the pieces of the puzzle fell into place in rewarding discussions and congruent viewpoints. There is a varied spatial sequence through the house, starting from the ceramics workshop behind the sauna lounge to the library above the living room.

The garage forms a separate unit along the road leading to the house. The main building was adapted to the terrain such that the kitchen-living room wing is perpendicular to the slope. This way the buildings could be located in the terrain as subtly as possible.

The buildings are built from aerated concrete blocks with a white render finish. The floors of the 208 m² dwelling are ceramic tiles and oak parquet flooring. The ceiling panels are built in common alder. The building has an under-floor hydronic heating system based on geothermal heating.

The interior décor includes family heirlooms inherited from the owner's grandfather, Alvar Aalto.

TAPANI MUSTONEN, ARCHITECT

PHOTOS ARNO DE LA CHAPELLE

The kitchen is situated a few steps above the living room. The living room floor is oiled oak and the ceiling common alder.

The light-filled bay window of the sauna suite overlooks the sheltered courtyard. The floors are clay tiles.

The sauna stove is heated from the side of the sauna lounge. Ria Alanen's ceramics studio can be seen in the background and on the wall in the foreground is a relief by her.

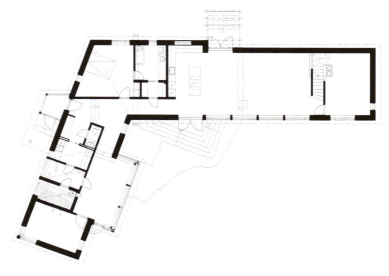

1:300

The southeast corner of the pistol-shaped house rises abruptly from the heathland. The courtyard is almost in its natural state: smooth rock outcrops, pine trees and natural meadow form an attractive and low maintenance totality.

1:1000

SADDLER'S COTTAGE
KANGASALA

The house, built amidst the lush landscape of Kangasala, is situated on the border between deciduous woodland and southwards-sloping cultivated farmland. The name of the house derived from a saddler's cottage that was previously on the site.

The ideals of the client couple, whose hobbies are gardening and culture, are linked with the classical tradition of architecture, which they became acquainted with already on trips to the Mediterranean countries during their student days. The two-storey rendered brick house is adjoined by a low car port in a seemingly arbitrary way. The massive front facade with its relief patterns, the tall wall projecting out from the facade, the natural stone embankment on the yard side and the red-tiled roof refer to the rural architecture of southern Europe to such an extent that the clients claimed that the house resembles one in Tuscany where it is claimed that Leonardo da Vinci met Mona Lisa.

The linear spatial sequence of the narrow-bodied house is made more spacious by a tall entrance hall with adjoining staircase and upper-storey balcony or loggia linked with the dining space. The floors are mainly light pine floor planks – from timber from the clients' own forest – and the walls are painted in different tones of yellow. The upstairs bedrooms have their own distinctive colours: blue, red, and rose pink.

KRISTIAN GULLICHSEN AND JYRI HAUKKAVAARA, ARCHITECTS

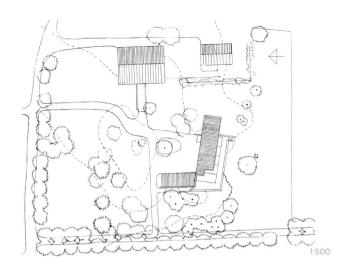

1:500

PHOTOS MAIJA HOLMA

The house was built in 1995 as a summer cottage but is now in year-round use. The floor area of the house is 268 m².

The entrance passage leading from the car port and storage through to the kitchen entrance.

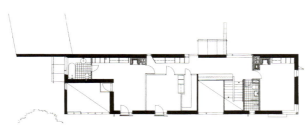

1ST FLOOR 1:400

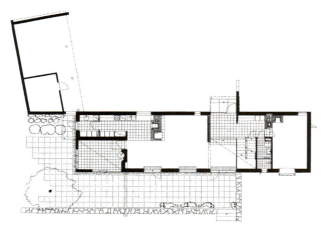

GROUND FLOOR 1:400

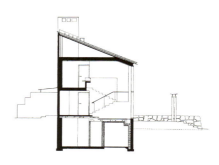

1:300

With its warm colours, the winter garden forms part of the autumn landscape.

The design of the house was accompanied by long stories about the histories of both Kangasala and Rome. The resultant house is an architectonic hybrid, in which Italian architettura minore and Nordic romantic modernism come together.

VILLA PAJUMÄKI
TUUSULA

The Nummenharju residential area in Tuusula is set in a landscape characterised by the imposing combination of a meadow-like parkland and a wilderness ridge. The landscape has been channelled to flow through the main spaces of the house. The V-shaped roof allows open views from the central hall and living room out to the landscape and has the same direction as the light entering the rooms.

The semi-atrium courtyard is an important feature in the series of spaces which emphasise the entrance and arrival home. A free-standing wall both protects the courtyard and demarcates the approach to the gate.

The bedrooms are at opposite ends of the house, each with its own distinct world. The kitchen receives the morning sun on the side of the house where the landscape is at its best. Also, there are strategic views from the kitchen to many of the other living spaces in the house. The common dining table is a continuation of the utility room and a place where one could actually work. The children's room can be subdivided in two different ways or combined with the utility room.

JUHA ILONEN, ARCHITECT

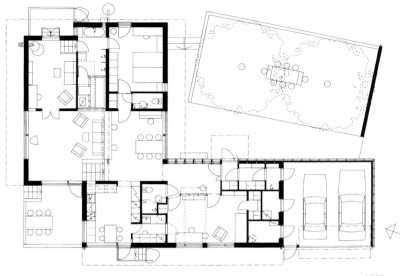

1:250

The landscape surrounding the house is a natural meadow. The shape of the roof was derived from the rooms opening out to the surroundings.

The atrium-courtyard, facing west, is the only area of lawn on the site. The louvres in the wall are set at 45 degrees to throw off snow and create a drip.

The east-west axis from the kitchen to the French balcony in the bedroom. There is a "look-out" window in the corner of the kitchen overlooking the living room. Villa Pajumäki was built in 2000 as an Artek design home for the Tuusula Housing Fair. The house has a floor area of 154 m^2.

HIENOVIRTA HOUSE
KAUNIAINEN

The home for a five-person family was built in an old residential area in Kauniainen in 2004, on a plot adjacent to a wooded park. The family wanted the house to be simple and bright. Thus the design is based on clearly defined spaces and surfaces.

The sauna and hobby spaces are situated in the cellar of the 236 m² house. The ground floor combined living and dining space looks out onto the garden via a large glazed wall. On the first floor are the bedrooms and a home office adjacent to an opening overlooking the space below.

Longitudinally the house is divided into three zones: a living and sleeping zone, the glass-roofed hall and the partly three-storey-high stairwell. Varying natural light floods through the rooflights, even into the centre of the house dominated visually by an eight-metre-tall exposed concrete wall.

The building structure consists of concrete blocks, in-situ cast concrete and steel columns. The intermediate concrete floor slabs are cast in-situ and the exterior facades have a rendered finish. Wide spruce planks have been used for the flooring of the living and dining space, while the basement has a varnished concrete floor.

YRJÄNÄ VUOJALA, ARCHITECT

PHOTOS MATTI KARJANOJA

From the outside the stairwell to the left of the entrance appears as a tall and narrow volume.

Natural light enters the shower area behind the partition of the sauna washroom from upper windows.

A wooden fence separates the private yard and concrete terrace from the main entrance. The interior contains Eero Aarnio designs: the Bubble Chair hanging from the ceiling and the Double Bubble floor lamp.

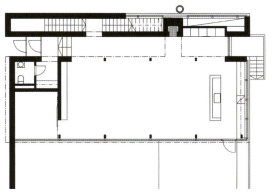

GROUND FLOOR 1:300

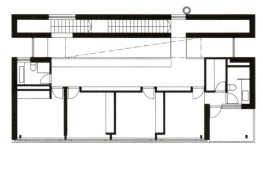

1ST FLOOR 1:300

TOIVIO HOUSE
HELSINKI

The 160 m² detached house I designed for my four-person family is located in a densely built old residential area in the Helsinki district of Jollas. In order to relieve the shortage of plots in the capital region, the spacious existing plots in the town plan could be divided up. Our small sloping rocky plot was parcelled out from the neighbouring plot. My aim was to create a peaceful yard milieu into which the different spaces of the house would open out to.

There are connections from all three floors of the house out into the surroundings. The main living areas and kitchen, with a vaulted ceiling, open out to the shady courtyard on the entrance level. There is access from the first floor bedroom to the sauna building via an upper yard. There are views over the treetops from the attic and roof terrace.

The main walls of the house are built in concrete blocks, and with a tinted rendered finish on the exterior. In the interior, the structural timbers of the intermediate floors and the roof have been left exposed. Interior finishes include birch, slate and ceramic tiles. The separate sauna building at the rear of the plot is built of logs treated with wood tar. The house was completed in 2006.

TEEMU TOIVIO, ARCHITECT

1:800

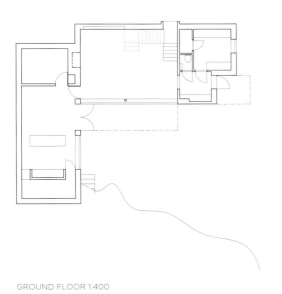

GROUND FLOOR 1:400

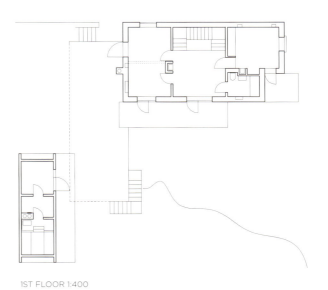

1ST FLOOR 1:400

HUMLEGÅRD HOUSE
FISKARS

The client wanted to move away from inner city Helsinki, to live all year round closer to nature. After a long search, a suitable plot was found at the eastern edge of an old village road a few kilometres from the centre of the old ironworks community of Fiskars, which in recent years has become a centre for culture. The house is located in the centre of its plot on a small hill at the edge of an overgrown glade and, following tradition, is oriented from corner to corner in a north-south direction.

The wooden monolithic dwelling can be seen as a typical peasant house split lengthways. The spruce-clad facade facing the village road is unassuming, in contrast to the tall galvanised corrugated-steel clad facade facing the lake, punctuated with large windows arranged freely to suit the interior space. The living spaces are divided into three multipurpose sections: two large rooms and a volume between them comprised of auxiliary spaces and, above these, a loft. The floor area of the house is 133 m².

After the completion of the main building, a combined woodshed and carport was built in the yard and a log sauna on the slope facing the lake.

KIMMO FRIMAN, ARCHITECT

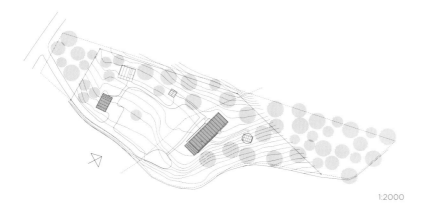

1:2000

The materials and colours were chosen jointly with the client, and as the building work progressed many building details were solved in similar discussions. The main interior walls and ceiling have been left untreated and await the patina of time. The birch plywood walls of the central volume have been painted with translucent egg-tempera: the orange bathroom, yellow-ochre walk-in wardrobe, the honey-coloured loft bathroom and the Prussian blue storage space have been surrounded by spring-green walls.

The room at the north end of the house, a few steps up from the rest of the ground floor, is dominated by a large atelier-like window. At work-table height there are windows in three directions. The steel stove adds to the ambience and provides an additional heat source.

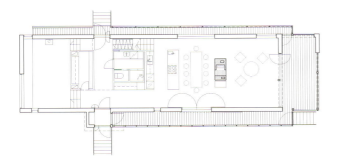

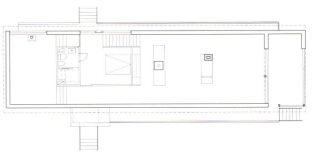

GROUND FLOOR 1:300

1ST FLOOR 1:300

183

At night-time the lit interior glows in the landscape like a lantern, and illuminates the nightly escapades of the white-tailed deer and foxes.

The double doors on the west facade in front of the dining space open up onto an uncovered terrace that runs along the side of the building. The view and amount of natural light can be regulated by the solid sliding door. There is direct access from the terrace to the yard. The spruce exterior weather-boarding is gradually turning grey.

The east façade of the house is clad with corrugated steel sheeting. The south end of the house – raised above the sloping site on concrete pillars and with a timber floor construction with a ventilated underspace – extends out into the open cultivated landscape. The cellar at the north end anchors the building to the slope. South of the house is an open expanse of field, on the west side is a yard delineated by outbuildings, and the east side overlooks a lake via a forested slope.

JUKKA KOSKINEN

On the east side of the house is a wood-heated log sauna, accessed via duckboards. The traditional-style spruce log frame was hewn in Hailuoto, north Finland, and built over a concrete well on the spot. The well was filled with absorbent gravel. The sauna door-hinges were custom forged by a local blacksmith. The actual sauna space is tall and it was important to place the benches on the same level as the sauna stove stones. The floor is a traditional simple wooden floor with a gradient, such that any water that has been thrown on the hot stones drains through an open gap in the floor. The space is ventilated by a hatch in the wall. Outside the sauna is a tap from where water is carried into the sauna in buckets. In winter the bathers can take a cooling roll in the fresh snow.

VILLA KARI
HELSINKI

The City of Helsinki offered disabled persons plots that were suitable for the construction of barrier-free homes. A family whose father uses a wheelchair obtained a plot in a traditional low-rise area and, having seen my earlier works, commissioned me to design a detached house for them.

I placed a garden in the middle of the plot, a piece of paradise, which the living spaces surround to form a circle. I wanted the wheelchair-bound resident to have free access to nature in all seasons.

The house appears to be formed from a number of rings: a terrace forms the outermost ring, connecting the house to the plot and allowing wheelchair access all around the house. The next ring is formed by the outer wall, which protects the house and garden from the gaze of passers-by. Next is the ring that forms the house's structural frame with its curved beams. The innermost circle is a curved glass wall that brings light into the house and connects the garden and interior.

The living room and kitchen form a single open space that continues out into the curved outdoor terrace. The more private spaces, such as the bedroom, bathroom and sauna, form their own demarcated elements along the outer wall of the house.

The house, with a floor area of 220 m², was assembled from prefabricated wood elements. It was completed in 2009.

OLAVI KOPONEN, ARCHITECT

1:300

PHOTOS JUSSI TIAINEN

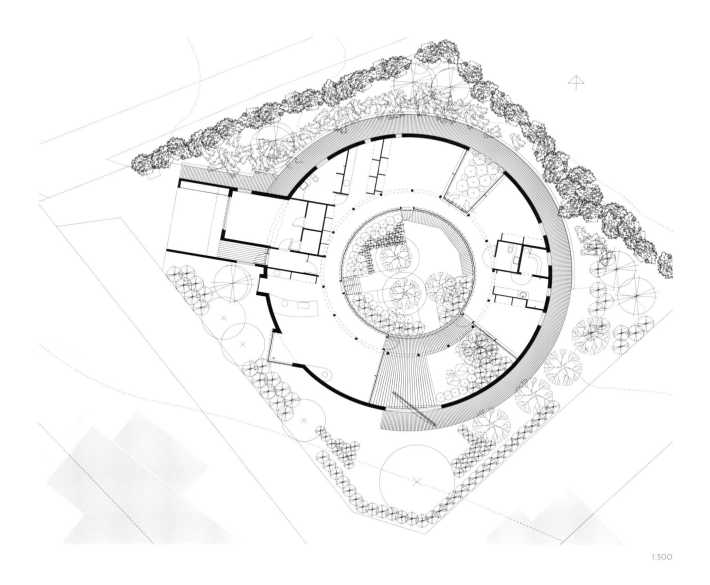

1:300

The lounge and kitchen together form a single space that encircles the garden at the centre of the house. The outdoor terrace is a continuation of the interior living spaces. On the inner ring of circles is a spacious route lined with columns. The ceiling made from thin light-coloured wood battens also follows the ring of circles, highlighting the continuity of the space. The house is heated by a geothermal pump and the heat pump of the air-conditioning unit, so that despite the abundance of glass surfaces it is still energy efficient.

The structure was assembled from wooden prefabricated elements and the exterior and interior cladding was carefully fitted on site. The vertical overlapping external boarding is larch. Due to its circular shape, the house stands out from its surroundings, but the wooden boarding, appropriate colour scheme and vegetation nevertheless help it to blend in.

The main entrance to the house is next to the garage, along a bright yellow corridor. The yellow is further emphasized by the light that falls through a round window. The corridor forms a contrast to the gentle wooden surfaces of the other interior spaces.

KOTI HOUSE
SIPOO

The house is situated on a steep eastern-facing slope. The plot is demarcated on the west side by the main road that cuts through the area and on the east side by a brook. There are tall fir trees growing on the upper part of the slope, while on the lower slope the vegetation changes to broad-leafed woodland.

The house was designed for two adults. It was completed in 2010, and has a floor area of 94 m^2. They spend their time there together or with friends and also sometimes work from home. The starting points in the design were their hobbies: plants, cooking and art. The rooms are linked together without a corridor, in an art gallery fashion. Space has been reserved for paintings and other artworks on the top-lit walls. The growing of plants has been concentrated in the over two-metre-deep plant box situated beneath the rooflight in the living room, where even large plants can thrive. The kitchen is located in the middle of the house and enables simultaneous social interaction and the preparation of food.

With the exception of the concrete block wall on the upper slope side, the house is built from timber. All surfaces are clad with wood panelling. The east facade is dominated by a glass wall that stretches along its entire length and which affords an extensive view down to the valley. The composition of the west facade is such that it appears as if the windows have been placed arbitrarily. The evening sun filters through these windows and they also provide views over the upper slope. A place has been reserved on the lower slope, near the brook, for a future sauna.

HEIKKI VIIRI, ARCHITECT

PHOTOS MIKA KASKINEN

The house is situated halfway up a slope, following the direction of the topography. The house rests on steel pillars on the lower side of the slope and on a concrete block wall on the upper side.

The sheltered terrace is accessible from both from the bedroom and main living spaces. From the terrace, a beautiful view opens up eastwards down the slope and southwards towards the sheltering forest.

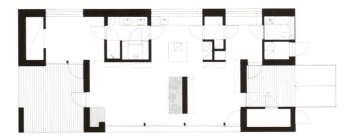

1:250

WIIMA HOUSE
ROVANIEMI

The house is located near Rovaniemi on a steep sloping site bordering the Kemijoki River. I drew up several different options for site layouts and, in discussion with the family, an array of three buildings was finally selected as a basis for further development.

Each of the three distinct building blocks – the garage, main building and waterfront sauna – is placed at a different angle along the path leading down to the river. I used this apparently haphazard layout in order to underline the natural state of the site.

The house is built mostly in wood. The 179 m² of floor space in the main building is distributed in rooms along a corridor extending the whole length of the building and stepped according to the inclination of the slope, before finally leading to a staircase down to the lower floor. One arrives at the house at a centrally placed hall that bisects the structure, separating quite naturally the residential functions. The uphill side of the house comprises the bedroom wing while on the downhill side is the sauna section, utility room and storage spaces. Above these are the living room, a large kitchen and a terrace, from where there is a view westwards towards the river.

HEIKKI VIIRI, ARCHITECT

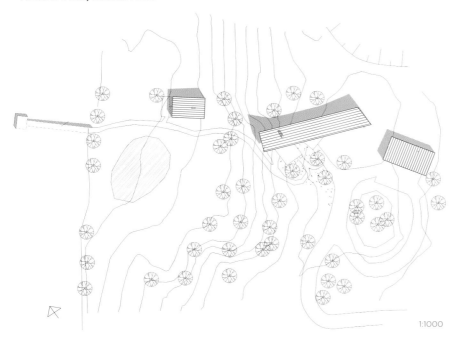

There is a view through the house towards the opposite shore of the Kemijoki river. A few steps lead from the kitchen to the living room. The kitchen-living room forms the core of the building. The wall-like cupboard provides plenty of storage space. On the wall above the table hangs 'Maria', a graphic print by Kuutti Lavonen. The flooring is common ash parquet glued to concrete. All interior walls and ceilings are clad in profiled wood panelling.

The main entrance is placed at the centre of the long south facade. The substantial mass placed across the slope gives the impression of a large building. The house was completed in 2008.

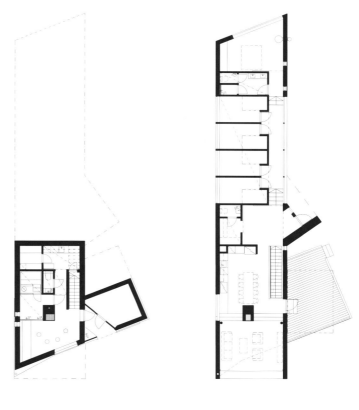

BASEMENT 1:300   GROUND FLOOR 1:300

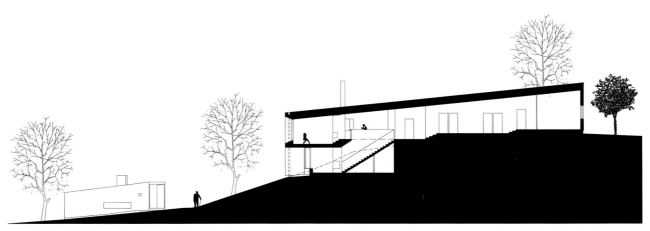

1:300

HOLAPPA HOUSE
ESPOO

I designed this white wooden house, with its starting point in the question of Finnish identity, as a home for friends returning to Finland after working abroad. The sheltered site in an area of old detached houses was parcelled off from a larger sloping plot. Part of the plot consists of protected deciduous woodland left in a natural state. The location of the house, sheltered from the gaze of passers-by, provided relative freedom in the design of the building's exterior. The house was completed in 2006.

The client's wishes for the rooms and the permissible floor area for the plot conflicted, as is often the case. The final design for the house became a compact entity on three floors with a total floor area of 147 m^2. The topmost floor comprises the main living areas, with beautiful views over the valley. The entrance hall and bedrooms are on the ground level, and the sauna and auxiliary spaces are in the basement.

The house is clad with painted timber battens. On three sides the battens are brought forward from the main wall plane, thus creating a sheltered terrace zone. There is access to the terrace from every room, and it plays an active role in everyday life in the house. It is even lit during the evening, so the house becomes a lantern, illuminating its surroundings.

PAVE MIKKONEN, ARCHITECT

On weekdays meals are taken in the kitchen, but which can extend, weather permitting, out on to the terrace on the north side of the house. The wall cladding is heat-treated wood, which is weather resistant and with very limited moisture movement.

BASEMENT 1:300

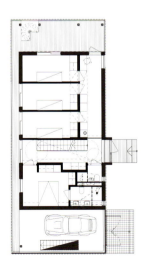

GROUND FLOOR 1:300

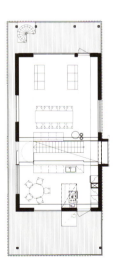

1ST FLOOR 1:300

3 TREES HOUSE
OULU

3 Trees House, which I designed for my own family, is a study of a contemporary courtyard setting consisting of three separate yards protected from the wind, and each containing a tree. The yards are demarcated by three sections: the wooden main building, a masonry wing and a carport. The landscape of the Kempele bay area and the narrow plot set the parameters for the layout of the spaces.

I maximised the landscape by placing the kitchen and living room on the upper floor of the main building. There is a direct connection from these spaces to the terrace situated on the roof of the wing building, which also includes an outdoor kitchen for summer use. On the ground floor of the main building are guest rooms and bedrooms, each of which has a connection to a terrace. The wing building contains a TV room, a sauna and utility spaces. The total floor area of the house is 260 m^2.

As the yard is sheltered from the wind, it is possible to spend time outdoors from early spring to late autumn in the sitting and dining areas on the terraces. Life moves around the house during the course of the day, from the sheltered moments during the morning in the yard to the sunsets over Kempele bay viewed from the roof terrace.

3 Trees House, completed in 2006, has been an experiment where I have been able to develop ideas that I would not have dared to try elsewhere.

PAVE MIKKONEN, ARCHITECT

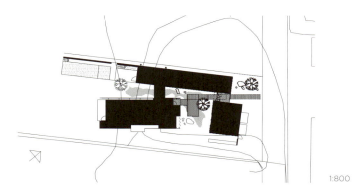

1:800

The kitchen worktop continues into the living room. Attached to the wall above it is a 12-metre-long artwork by artist Markku Kolehmainen.

The kitchen, dining area and living room overlook Kempele Bay and the Gulf of Bothnia. There is direct access from the kitchen to the roof terrace above the sauna.

The facades of the main building are clad with oil-painted spruce weatherboarding and plywood.

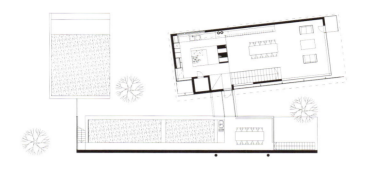

1ST FLOOR 1:400

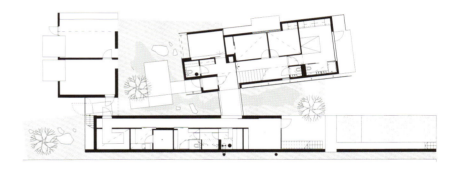

GROUND FLOOR 1:400

PHOTOS A.-P. PIESKÄ

'TOUCH' HOUSE

'Touch' is a single-family house intended for industrial manufacture, and individual examples of which have already been built in different locations. The aim was to create a prefabricated house suitable for an urban environment, an alternative to the manor-house-style that dominates the market. As it is intended for a four-person family, it was reckoned that just over 140 m² of net floor area would be needed.

Despite the building's clearly defined exterior, the interior comprises a variety of forms. The mono-pitched roof forms a four-cornered compact envelope around a series of varied private outdoor spaces. The otherwise tiled roof has glazed sections above the veranda, bedroom balcony, and sauna terrace, bringing light into the middle of the building frame.

One gets a sense of the spatial layout of the house already at the entrance. Vistas can open longitudinally and transversally in the building, depending on the plot and the landscape.

The rooms are grouped around a 1½ -storey open 'farmhouse'-type living area, which is centred on the "hearth", which would be either a masonry fireplace built on site or a standard steel stove. The main room comprises a living space, kitchen, and dining area, each marked by furniture within the space of varying height. The exterior wall follows freely the floor plan beneath a uniform roof plane, which allows for the positioning of windows in three directions in most of the rooms.

'Touch' has been designed on the basis of the manufacturer's production technology. The house is made from large prefabricated elements assembled and surface finished in the factory. The facade grills and horizontal battens are installed on site as separate elements.

Additional space can be achieved when needed by inserting an upper floor on top of the entrance hall or sauna porch. It is also possible to convert the garage into a small separate flat.

MIKKO HEIKKINEN AND MARKKU KOMONEN, ARCHITECTS

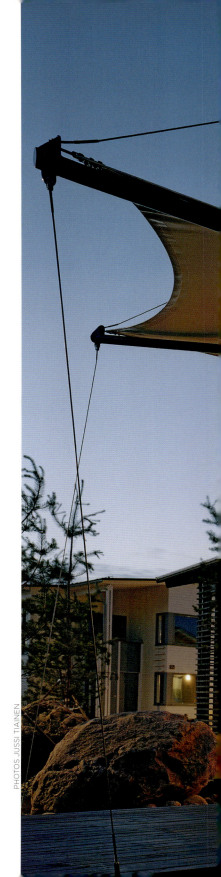

PHOTOS: JUSSI TIAINEN

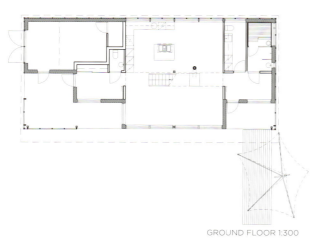

GROUND FLOOR 1:300

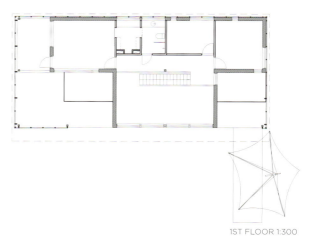

1ST FLOOR 1:300

The prototype of the Touch house was displayed at the Tuusula Housing Fair in 2000. The house has a clearly defined and compact exterior, yet is spatially diverse in the interior. Sheltered under the same roof are various outdoor spaces which are overlooked from the different rooms of the house. The bedrooms at each end of the house have windows facing at least two directions. The exterior spaces "inside" the house receive light through glazed sections of the tiled roof.

The basic design of the standardised house can be adapted according to the needs of the client and the terrain and local detailed plan, as evident in the example built in Marjaniemi, Helsinki, in 2000. The room layout and construction are similar to the prototype at the Tuusula Housing Fair, but a different colour scheme and surroundings change the mood of the house. The garage in the prototype has here now in this case become a hobby room.

DOMUS ARBOREA
HELSINKI

The house, originally designed and built as the architect family's home, is located in Tapanila in north-east Helsinki. The 550 m² site had been parcelled off from the plot of the neighbouring vernacular Jugendstil house. Inspiration for the design of the house was derived from the context, and in turn the completed building complements the existing urban fabric. In particular, the design was influenced by the nearby Tapanila Workers Club dating from the end of the 1940s and beginning of the 1950s.

The design was also based largely on ecological principles. The materials are characterised by a restrained aesthetic and are nearly all natural; for instance, impregnated wood was used only in those structures of the outdoor terrace that are close to the ground.

Due to the municipal infrastructure that cuts through the site, the main entrance is placed at the corner and one enters via a semi-heated vestibule. The main room on the ground floor is an open kitchen partly bordered by a double storey height dining space. Natural light enters the bright rooms from mainly two directions. The bedrooms and sauna were placed on the upper floor and the sauna terrace above the entrance hall. A well-lit home office space – which could also serve as a separate flat – was placed in the half-sunk basement floor.

VESA PEKKA ERIKKILÄ AND MARJUT KAUPPINEN, ARCHITECTS

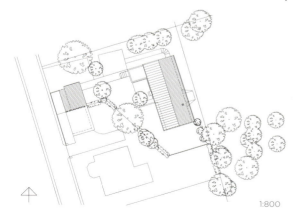

1:800

Many of the building parts, including the hand-built kitchen sink unit, cooker hood, interior stairs, bathroom cabinets and even the WC door signs were specially designed for this house.

The grey-coloured house with its simple lines is sited immediately adjacent to a park, and in places you can see right through the slender building. The simple, pleasant house, built in 2003, resembles the traditional houses from the 1950s that exist in the area.

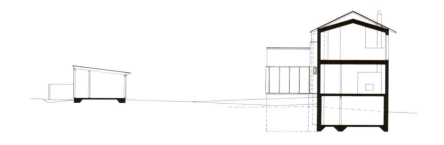

1:600

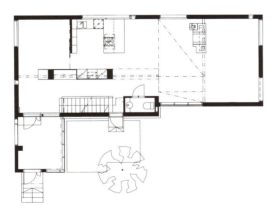

GROUND FLOOR - 1:600

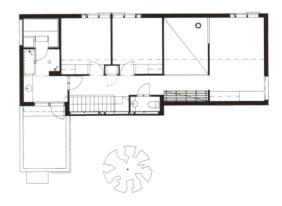

1ST FLOOR 1:600

VILLA NIINIMÄKI
OULU

When designing an efficient and functional narrow-plan house in the Toppila harbour area of Oulu we could not avoid the mental image of a boat.

The organisation of the functions in the two-storey 220 m² house was guided by the flow of the landscape and natural light. The ground floor bedrooms receive morning sunlight. The sauna suite, which faces west, bathing in the evening sun, is separated from the main building mass by a sauna lounge and a terrace above. On the first floor, the living room, under a high ceiling that follows the slants of the pitched-roof, and the dining and kitchen spaces, made intimate by a gallery space above, have extensive views of the surrounding landscape and receive plenty of natural light due to the narrow frame of the building. On ascending from the dimly lit ground floor to the light of the first floor, one feels as if one is standing on the deck of a ship, looking out to sea.

TEIJU AUTIO AND SEEPO SEROLA, ARCHITECTS

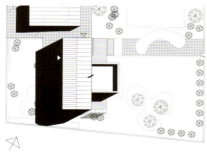

1:800

The strip windows on either side of the house orient the dining area and kitchen towards both the morning and evening sun. When standing at the kitchen island you feel as if you are on the captain's bridge of a ship. The use of timber, dark blue colour, railings and intense contrasts of light all bear reference to seaside landscapes. The house was completed in 2005.

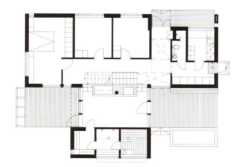

GROUND FLOOR 1:300

1ST FLOOR 1:300

Harri Hautajärvi is a Helsinki architect who has run his own office since 1995, designing interiors, exhibitions and buildings. He has also made art installations and participated in exhibitions. Hautajärvi has written numerous articles on architecture for journals and books as well as lectured on architecture both in Finland and abroad. He was editor-in-chief of the journal *Arkkitehti – The Finnish Architectural Review* between 2000 and 2008, during which time he and the journal received several awards, including the Pierre Vago Award for Architectural Journalism in 2003 from The International Committee of Architectural Critics CICA and the Alfred Kordelin Foundation Incentive Award for 2005. Hautajärvi was awarded the Finnish Periodical Publishers' Association award in 2007 for the best editorial and the Yhdyskuntasuunnittelun Ruusu [Urban Planning Rose] award in 2008.

Harri Hautajärvi's previous book, **Villas and Saunas in Finland**, from 2010, presented 48 summer villas and saunas, from the marine archipelago to the lake district and fells of the north. In addition to the individual building presentations, Hautajärvi writes about the history of Finnish summer house and sauna culture, as well offering examples of energy-saving and low-carbon solutions for summer houses. Photo: Architect Olavi Koponen's Villa Långbo.

The first edition of *Villas and Saunas in Finland* was a long list nominee for the Sir Nikolaus Pevsner RIBA International Book Award for Architecture 2007.